Also by Miriam Weinstein

Prophets & Dreamers:
A Selection of Great Yiddish Literature

Yiddish: A Nation of Words

The

SURPRISING POWER

of

FAMILY MEALS

The
SURPRISING POWER
of
FAMILY MEALS

How Eating Together
Makes Us Smarter, Stronger,
Healthier, and Happier

MIRIAM WEINSTEIN

STEERFORTH PRESS
HANOVER, NEW HAMPSHIRE

For information about permission to reproduce
selections from this book, write to:
Steerforth Press L.C., 25 Lebanon Street,
Hanover, New Hampshire 03755

Library of Congress Cataloging-in-Publication Data

Weinstein, Miriam.
  The surprising power of family meals : how eating together makes us
smarter, stronger, healthier, and happier / Miriam Weinstein. — 1st ed.
    p. cm.
  Includes bibliographical references.
  ISBN 1-58642-092-5 (alk. paper)
  1. Family. 2. Dinners and dining — Social aspects. 3. Dinners and dining —
Psychological aspects. I. Title.
  HQ734.W4376 2005
  306.85—dc22

                                  2005010191

FIRST EDITION

"It seems to me that our three basic needs, for food and security and love, are so mixed and mingled and entwined that we cannot straightly think of one without the others. So it happens that when I write of hunger, I am really writing about love and the hunger for it, and warmth and the love of it and the hunger for it . . . and then the warmth and richness and fine reality of hunger satisfied . . . and it is all one."

M. F. K. Fisher, *The Art of Eating*

"I know that young children will wander away from the table, and that family life is never smooth, and that life itself is full, not only of charm and warmth and comfort but of sorrow and tears. But whether we are happy or sad, we must be fed. Both happy and sad people can be cheered up by a nice meal."

Laurie Colwin, *Home Cooking*

For Peter, my favorite supper companion

— ACKNOWLEDGMENTS —

I have so many people to thank: people who have cared about the topic, or about me. There were people who didn't know me from Adam or Eve, but took time to answer my questions and then go beyond them, helping me to better chart my course.

My agent, Sally Brady, has been a smart, caring coach as I figured out what this book was about, and then helped me make it happen. My two writing groups — Alice Holstein, Glenn Morrow, Sherry Nadworny, Mike Scott — and Jeanne Guillemin, Cindy Linkas, Karen McQuillan, Patricia Welbourn — held my hand through all the ups and downs. Betsy Seifter, particularly, has talked me through many drafts.

A special thanks to the folks in Wayzata, Minnesota, especially Barbara Carlson, for going way beyond any reasonable expectation of how to welcome a stranger.

Thanks to Steerforth Press, especially Chip Fleischer, for taking a gamble on this idea. Robin Dutcher, Pia Needham, Kristin Sperber, Louise Fili, Laura Jorstad, and Helga Schmidt all did their expected excellent jobs.

And thanks to every one of these: Madeleine Abrams, Brad Anderson, Harry Balzer, Carol Bergenstal, Betsy Christopherson, Jillian Croll, Kate Culhane, Kerry Daly, Denny Dart, Henrietta Davis, Bill Doherty, Marshall Duke, Lei-Anne Ellis, David Englander, Judy Englander, Greg Fedio, Susan Feinstein, John Finn, Phyllis Fischer, Robyn Fivush, Lynn Fredericks, David Gaither, Matthew Gillman, Lili Gottfried, Jane Guffy, Rosalie Harrington, Andy Harris,

John Hogenson, Bill Huebsch, Evan Imber-Black, Anne Johnson and family, Sue Kakuk and family, Paul Kelly, Anna Kovel, Maureen Lahr, Jessica Lamothe, Amber Lazarus, Allison Lee, Jennie Leszkiewicz, Marion Lindblad-Goldberg, Marcia Marra, Miriam Meyers, Sidney Mintz, Wendy Mogel, Julie Mowery, Dianne Neumark-Sztainer, Kim Pedersen, Bugs Peterschmidt, Julie Pfitzinger, Ellen Rafel, Laura Roberto-Forman, Franco Romagnoli, Gwen Romagnoli, Paul Rozin, Rose Rubin, Sara Rubin, Witold Rybczynski, Peter Sack, Zoe Sanders, Ellyn Satter, Cindy Schallock, Bradd Shore, Alexandra Siemon, Catherine Snow, Ceci Snyder, Lauren Swann, Peter Steinglass, Patton Tabors, Caitlin Thomas-Lepore, Marcia Treno, Bertrand Weber, Jon Weiner, Sharon Weiss-Kapp, Susan Whitehead, Joan Wickersham, Alice Woog, the folks at the Manchester Public Library, and the folks at the Schlesinger Library.

I would like to thank my dog, Sully, who followed me up and down the stairs a million times and tried not to bark during phone interviews. I remember my parents, Saul and Sally Weinstein, who created the iconic childhood suppers I shared with my sister, Naomi. I would like to thank my children, Eli and Mirka Feinstein, for years and years of lively meals. My husband, Peter Feinstein, has always been an appreciative eater and supportive spouse.

I am immensely grateful to you all.

— CONTENTS —

Well, Magic Enough . . .

WHAT IF I told you that there *was* a magic bullet — something that would improve the quality of your daily life, your children's chances of success in the world, your family's health, our values as a society? Something that is inexpensive, simple to produce, and within the reach of pretty much everyone?

Then, after you had me committed to the Asylum for the Incurably Optimistic, you might come and visit me from time to time. And while you were there, if you were lucky, I would invite you to join me and my fellow inmates for supper.

Over a leisurely, delicious meal (remember, we optimists have our eye on life's glories), we would talk about the research that's been accumulating from very, very disparate fields. It shows how eating ordinary, average everyday supper with your family is strongly linked to lower incidence of bad outcomes such as teenage drug and alcohol use, and to good qualities like emotional stability. It correlates with kindergarteners being better prepared to learn to read. (It even trumps getting read to.) Regular family supper helps keep asthmatic kids out of hospitals. It discourages both obesity and eating disorders. It supports your staying more connected to your extended family, your ethnic heritage, your community of faith. It will help children and families to be more resilient, reacting positively to those curves and arrows that life throws our way. It will certainly keep you better nourished. The things we are likely to discuss at the supper table anchor our children more firmly in the world. Of course eating together teaches manners both trivial and momentous, putting you in touch with the deeper springs of human relations.

When families prepare meals together, kids learn real-life skills. They assume responsibility, become better team members. (Where did we get the idea that the only teams are in sports?) Sharing meals helps cement family relationships, no matter how you define *family*. The word *companion*, which dates back to ancient Rome, means "one who breaks bread with you."

One thing family supper does not do: It does not correlate with higher rates of winning Merit Scholarships. That's an urban legend that is quoted with nodding certainty by high school principals at the start of every school year. It might actually be true, but it has never been tested. Still, it makes intuitive sense, which is why this particular myth lives on. Aside from the scholarship link, though, all the other good things you have ever thought about plain old family suppers (or dinners; for our purposes the same thing) are probably true. And the best part of all is that you should do these things not just because they are good for you, but because they *feel* good. The immediate goal here is for your family to get more genuine pleasure out of being together. When that happens, the other benefits will follow.

Because I want you to share my optimism about what you can expect from your family meals and, by extension, from your family, I invite you to come along with me to a Minnesota town where parents are doing their best to regain some purchase on family life; to a New Jersey community that is quite realistic about the enormity of a similar task. Together, we will see what family supper means for anorexics, theologians, family therapists. We're going to travel far afield, delving into linguistics, psychology, urban sociology, and history, while always keeping the family table front and center. ' We will see young parents who are hemorrhaging time, literally running to pick up their little ones from day care; then we will discover what every household can learn from the single-parent model. We will find out more ways that TV undermines the job that loving parents try to do. Above all, we will keep an eye on what is well within our power to effect, both in our own homes and in the world beyond.

One image I have of supper comes from my early twenties, when I got to spend some nontouristy time with Parisian families. The women all had jobs, but for men and women alike, work ended promptly at five, with evenings sacred to family and friends. The kids would come home from a full day at school and start their homework. On her way home from work, Renee, the mother in the household I came to know best, would stop at the market and pick up fresh meat, bright vegetables, bread baked that afternoon.

As a foreign visitor with uncertain culinary skills, I was given only simple chores — soaking the loose-leafed lettuce in a bowl of water to wash out the dirt, and then putting the lettuce in a wire basket and swinging it in circles out over the tiny balcony, the droplets of water forming an arc in the oh-so-Parisian summer air.

Dinner began at seven or so, a leisurely affair fueled by

conversation and the pleasure of being together, guests and family. The food was superfresh and tasty, with many separate courses that were, by current American standards, minute — a perfect slice of melon topped with a paper-thin glint of ham; a single flat cutlet; a helping of shiny (very thin, of course) green beans. For the French, in addition to the preparation and the freshness, it is the ensemble that counts; the way the courses fit together. The salad (modestly sized, with no cucumbers, carrots, peppers, or sprouts, no greasy croutons from a vacuum-sealed bag) comes after the meal, a palate cleanser before the creamy richness of the cheese course, which often serves as dessert. (So, you notice, the cook is able to present three courses while actually cooking only one.)

And the ensemble of people could shine as well: the variety of ages and opinions juxtaposed, sometimes melding, sometimes contrasting, but making, together, a humanoid whole. The kids had their place in the family; the family had its place in the world. Dinner had its place in the cycle of the day — a time for sitting back, for winding down, just as the fruits and vegetables that appeared in the neighborhood market served to mark the seasons of the year.

This is what I remember now: a wholeness, a balance; everyone sitting around the table talking or laughing or arguing or just listening, feeling comfy with the good food and the wine. The kids (*les gosses*, two sons at that awkward junior high school age) mostly just took it all in. They drank diluted wine; they cut their fruit into neat squares with fork and knife, eating whatever was on their plates.

Their parents didn't worry about the kids not liking what was served, being bored or behind in their schoolwork or out of touch with their friends. After a long day at school, they weren't subjected to a spiraling round of lessons, practices, meetings, and games; their parents and siblings weren't subjected to the requisite chauffering, waiting, and cheering. It was assumed that the kids would learn something from meeting a variety of informed, chatty people in a relaxed setting; that in time they would grow up to become friendly and civil and balanced and well informed themselves, able to take part in the give-and-take of cultured people, capable of discriminating between a pear, or an argument, that was ripe and one that was still green.

My discovery of Paris was not exactly unique. Along with thousands of young Americans, I came home from my Eurail Pass summer ready to demand crusty baguettes, rich, soft cheeses, and a decent glass of inexpensive wine.

Well, we have them all now, but look what we've done with them. As any anthropologist will tell you, it's one thing for a culture to borrow an artifact; it's something quite different to incorporate an attitude or worldview. We think it's funny when a jungle tribe takes the visiting anthropologist's used batteries and fashions them into necklaces. But we've done the same thing ourselves.

Americans by the wide-bodied-plane load have discovered the wonders of carefully prepared, fresh, and flavorful foods. We've replaced our spongy packaged white bread with the best that Paris has to offer. Well, sort of. We've skipped the part about stopping into the neighborhood *boulangerie* and exchanging courtesies with Madame. We've gone right to the part where we have our baguettes any way a demanding consumer might want them — flash frozen, whole wheat, mini and maxi, already covered with sauce and cheese for ersatz pizzas perfect for snacking. They sit, shrink wrapped, in our enormous freezers for months on end. We can eat them any-time we like, without waiting for the burden of human com-panionship. If the breads are rubbery and prone to freezer burn, we don't complain; that's the price we're happy to pay for instant, impersonal access.

We got the news about wanting to eat food that tastes good. But somewhere, as my daughter would say, we missed the memo about the pleasures of making it and eating it and sharing it with people we care about. We've perfected the segmentation of the family. Nobody has to eat the same food, watch the same show, listen to the same song, let alone sing it. We love to imagine the French with their lush tables, or the Italians with their big families, but we prefer to gobble our take-out, our home delivery, our single-serve microwave, on the run, in front of the TV, in the food court, or in the car, while we dream of quality time, of family vacations, of some-place far away.

Sure, there have always been variations on the supper theme. In many patriarchal societies, the women serve the men, then eat with the children or only after everyone else has finished, picking at scraps. But we are talking in a general way about an institution — the shared primary meal — that is multiethnic, multicultural, multi- most things across the sweep of human history. Certainly, it has been a feature of our Western civiliza-tion for centuries. But somehow, while no one was looking, this most widespread way of relating has gone into a steep and dra-matic decline. Breaking bread, reaching our chopsticks into the communal bowl of stir-fry, using our hands, or chapati, or banana leaf to scoop up the goodness our loved ones have labored over, seems to be in danger of extinction in the U.S. of A.

As does talking while we do it; sharing news of what happened that day in the office, around the house, at day care or school. Shushing our children, or encouraging them to talk. Arguing politics, gossiping, trading jokes, ideas, or tall tales. It is the rapid decline of family suppers, the enormity of the potential loss, that has propelled me to write this book.

As I have gone about my life during the process, I've met lots of people — at parties, at the grocery store, at the transfer station (no longer called the town dump). Here's what happens when I tell them I'm what working on: Sometimes, if the people are around my age (empty-nester), they will tell me, with great feeling and pride, that the family made a point of having supper (every night/as often as they could) when the kids were at home, and they are so glad they did. Most often, though, whatever their age, they will launch into a spirited description of supper in their own childhood home. It doesn't matter whether they are eight or eighty; they want to give me a detailed scenario of the tone, the setting, the rules, of the everyday, ordinary, repetitive suppers of their youth.

Most often this is told with great loyalty and affection. *We always ate this; my brother sat there; boy, did we kids love to . . .* Occasionally, this recital is tinged with fury. *My mother insisted; my father forced us kids . . .* But I am amazed at the small percentage of bad meal memories I encounter, and the strength of the recall, the sense of how much those meals shaped the person before me. *We always . . . Every night we . . . For a treat we would . . .* This is not a question of haute cuisine or shocking emotional revelations or brilliant analyses of world events, but rather a no-big-deal time when kids can count on seeing their parents, and parents know they can spend a bit of time with their kids. Even siblings will sometimes admit to feeling more secure, knowing that they will all be together at regular intervals with no particular agenda other than filling their bellies and checking in. What counts is the sitting around together, sharing life, doing what families do.

Or do they? On this topic, contemporary statistics are all over the place, depending on your definition of *family*, or *supper*, or *together*. You can find statistics that say that hardly anyone is eating together, or that a hefty majority are. (In those studies, we have to be aware of the tendency of people to tell interviewers what they want to hear; to make themselves sound a bit better than they are.) You also have to be careful about how the asker is framing the question: If everyone takes a helping of the same meal, but then retreats to eat it alone, in the bedroom, in front of the TV, does that count? How about if a couple of family members sit down together but eat different, prepackaged things? What if everyone sits and eats, but one kid is wearing a headset while another is instant-messaging friends?

My sense is that, without much thought, we have let this basic human ritual slide to the point where it has dropped below critical mass. In the United States, across class, race, and economic lines, everyday family supper is no longer a given. Staff members of an eating disorders clinic have told me that the anorexics they work with rarely know how to set a table. Cause or effect? You can argue that it's both. I met a woman in Minnesota who was shocked to discover that the nice middle-class family next door did not even own a dining room or kitchen table. I was surprised as well, the first time I heard that kind of report. Now I just nod.

Here is what I see: Because, as a society, we do not favor

supper with preferential treatment, because we schedule everything constantly, all the time, that humble shared meal is no longer expected. And because it is not expected, it is less likely to happen. And so it is expected even less. We stay late at the office. We stop by the gym, or catch up on our e-mail. We drive one kid to soccer, and bring another one along in the car. (According to a recent study by the University of Michigan Survey Research Center, between 1981 and 1997 the time that children spent watching other people, like siblings, play sports rose fivefold.)

We grab fast food, or let the kids open the freezer and fend for themselves. Our supermarket aisles are bulging with single-serving, idiot-proof, heat-and-eat meal substitutes. And the more of them we buy, the less practice we have in putting meals together. Who even knows what *a meal* means? How do we learn what constitutes a reasonable portion, what tastes good, what our grandmothers cooked, what we should combine with what to make a tasty, nutritionally complete, appealing whole?

We are living in a time of intense individualism, in a culture defined by competition and consumption. It has become an article of faith that a parent's job is to provide every child with every opportunity to find his particular talent, interest, or bliss. But somehow, as we drive-thru our lives, we have given up something so modest, so humble, so available, that we never realized its worth. Family supper can be a bulwark against the pressures we all face every day.

And no, I am not advocating a return to some Neverland of meat loaf and ruffled aprons. If an institution is anywhere near as good as I'm saying supper is, it must be flexible, reflecting who we are at this time in our culture, in our lives.

Today's supper will not be like yesterday's. Except that, in terms of meeting basic human needs, it will be. It will be much the same as the long-ago time our ancestors squatted around the campfire in front of the cave and doled out pieces of nicely charred venison accompanied by fresh-picked berries, and retold the story of the day's hunt.

At my own house these days, supper is rather quiet: just my husband and me and our arthritic, deaf dog. We eat lots of fish and fresh veggies. If you had come by for supper ten or twenty years ago, you would have found a raucous scene, and been offered something like hamburger and cheese grits, or maybe bangers and mash. In my own 1950s childhood, suppers tended toward plain broiled chops and canned veggies, and were timed to my father's schedule. He was an old-fashioned doctor with evening office hours. We ate counting the minutes to the time he had to walk downstairs to a full waiting room. My mother, who had been a nurse, was desperate to get back to work after we kids were born. But my father saw her working as an insult to his ability to provide. So my mom changed careers, took a job at the far end of the subway line, and dashed home to get supper on the table on time. When she didn't make it, my sister and I, from age ten or so on, would run around the corner to Joe the butcher, heat up the canned zucchini, broil the chops.

In my parents' difficult marriage, supper was a calm spot in the day. Discussion of cases and diagnoses, tumors that always seemed to be as big as grapefruit, never diminished anyone's appetite, although my father might note that I would never make it to the clean plate club. See what I mean about the suppers of our childhood? I dare you to boil yours down to a sentence or two. (Can't I just tell you about the way I would lift our dainty little black pug onto my lap so she could join in the after-dinner conversation?)

Nowadays, in magazines and in TV commercials, cooking wonderful food for our loved ones is presented as misery, or at best an irksome chore. Whereas sitting in traffic so we can stand in line to grab a wrapped-up, standardized, nutritionally questionable meal (what do they really care about — your waistline or their bottom line?) to be swallowed as quickly as possible before getting back in the car again is fun! A treat! A break we deserve! We have managed to convince ourselves that hanging out in the kitchen for an hour with our kids, siblings, or parents — chopping, eating, cleaning up, all accompanied by the ebb and flow of daily chatter — is demeaning, embarrassing, not worth our time.

We have made our busyness a form of conspicuous consumption. Women (and it is still primarily women) face increasingly higher expectations for child rearing, as well as ever-larger homes. They are expected to maintain their own looks and health to stringent standards, and all this while pursuing interesting and lucrative careers. (My gosh, I didn't even mention the need to maintain a perfect love relationship.) Who has time for supper?

Well, you do. Your family does. We all do. Believe me, I would not be making such a big deal about supper if we had other, stronger communal bonds. But we are living in a time when the social fabric is fraying, and supper is one of the few habits that has not yet disappeared from memory.

So what do you recall of your own childhood suppers? How did they shape you? What would you like to pass along; what would you definitely change? Now ask yourself: When your children are your age, what memories will they have? Do chicken fingers and fries eaten in the backseat of the car count as a meal? Do notes on the fridge substitute for conversation?

Research shows that even families who are toxic, dysfunctional, awful, do better if they can maintain rituals such as supper. Families who are anything approaching "normal" get dividends from their rituals far down the line. Cause or effect, you might ask; chicken or egg? Maybe families who eat together are just more organized, or loving, or effective from the get-go.

I say, Why worry? Learn what it is about supper that makes it so powerful. If you aren't doing it, give it a try. If you are doing it, do it with more intention, more awareness, more verve, more fun. Whatever your starting point, whatever the size or composition of your family, let supper work its magic for you. Think, for a moment, about what you really want for your clan. Is it yet more time in the car? Or would you rather enjoy each other, be more of what you hoped a family would be?

Supper is about nourishment of all kinds. Don't be bashful, don't rush off. Come to the table. Enjoy the food and each other. Let yourself dig in.

— 2 —

Making the Frame

IT HELPS TO imagine an ornate gold frame. Pick it up (don't worry; it's only pretend) and place it around the image that appears when you say "supper at my house." Bet the picture you see is very specific: *These are the seats we sit in, the things we discuss. Here is the person who shows up last. That is the bowl we use for the rice.*

When I began this book, it had never occurred to me that supper is a ritual. That was a concept I had associated with exotica, religion, or at least Big Things. I could not have been more wrong. Once I got a sense of the importance of ordinary, everyday rituals (and supper is the one most often cited), I could understand the strength that comes from this evening meal.

Inside your imaginary frame, your table and the people around it come into focus, while the area beyond it falls away. Just so, ritual sets the actors and their actions apart from the surrounding space and time, bumping everything up a notch, infusing habit with meaning. I am not saying that your teenager's tantrum or your seven-year-old's interminable recitation of a playground contretemps is religious or holy. I'm talking about a kind of everyday secular sacredness.

It's the way that, as you dash to the table with your barely-made-it-in-time platter of reheated or thrown-together-at-the-last-minute *whatever*, you can see everyone there, just as they are tonight and never will be again.

Ritual sets ordinary gestures and events into bold relief. Those simple actions that get repeated night after night become the road maps of our lives. They point us toward home, the footprints in the snow. Setting our feet in those preformed places is so much easier than breaking new trail.

Social scientists talk about how ritual intensifies the emotional interaction of the participants; how it increases their sense of purpose. They mention "props" or significant objects, as well as following a "script." In one family, napkins are always put on laps before anyone begins. The parent in such a family nods toward a folded white napkin that has not found its way onto the appropriate lap, raises eyebrows and intones the singsong reminder, "White sails in the sunset." In another family, pie is never served without a scoop of ice cream.

In the white-sails family, kids know they're supposed to put their napkins on their laps as soon as they sit down. They know they can get a rise out of their parent if they don't. In the dessert family, everyone knows that pie comes with ice cream. If, one night, the pie arrives naked, someone will grab a fork and complain, because something in that cosmos has shifted.

Ritual is about boundaries and transitions, easing us from one time, or activity, or mood, to another. And because we do the same thing again and again and again, it forms the thin and permeable line between stability and change. Because we have things that we always do, we don't have to invent them night after night. Then, when we strike out in a new direction — clearing the table without being asked, or staying in our seat when we usually jump up to clear — it stands out in bold relief. How do we experience sickness or argument or business pressure or divorce? Nothing speaks louder than an empty chair.

Rituals illustrate what we believe. That white-sails jingle lets us know that this family cares about form. The ice cream with pie shows us a family who enjoys its food, or isn't concerned about calories, or is active and needs to replenish its nutritional stores. Or maybe it believes in the curative power of ice cream.

The currency of ritual is separation. We separate ourselves from other people, other activities. We join together, however briefly, to form a supper group. Sitting down to a meal together draws a line around us. It encloses us and, for a brief time, strengthens the bonds that connect us with the other members of our self-defined clan, shutting out the rest of the world.

The more we are conscious of this ritual frame, this imaginary boundary line, the more it can help us. We can tweak our rituals, scrap those that don't work, begin new, more satisfying ones. We can decide if our family is too bounded by rituals in general — like children squeezing into clothing that they have outgrown. Or we may not have ritual enough, and we are left shivering.

Some aspects of ritual are set in stone, while others are fluid as water. The closed parts, like the repetition of the same blessing or grace every night, express our values, link us to our histories. The way we sit, the time of day we gather for our main meal, our choice of foods, echo the things that many of our friends and neighbors are doing at more or less the same time. Even though I have fancied up many of my food habits since childhood, I still most often begin supper with a slice of melon or half a grapefruit, cut just the way my mother did it. How many Americans, living overseas, suddenly find themselves toward the end of November scrounging for something resembling turkey? All around the globe, expats seek each other out, preparing faux Thanksgiving meals, substituting lingonberry jam for cranberry sauce, chicken or goose for the unavailable bird.

And the open parts of ritual? They let us shift, restructure, invent. Really good rituals work in more than one way, with symbolic actions sneaking in under the skin. Joining hands together as we say grace; having a small child bring her beloved stuffed animal to the table and set it carefully beside her; using Grandma's old china — these kinds of gestures take on meanings beyond themselves.

Above all, rituals give form to relationships. A hundred years ago, before mass entertainment, when New England townsfolk wanted to mark a holiday or anniversary they created what they called tableaux vivants, living pictures. People would dress up in costumes and compose themselves into reenactments — what we might think of as freeze frames — while their neighbors looked on. Where I live, the favorites were the arrival of the first ship in Salem Harbor and the meeting with Chief Massasoit. On the "ship," the newcomers would all be scanning the horizon for their first glimpse of land; at the "meeting," the chief and the captain occupied center stage, saluting each other with appropriate dignity, each surrounded by a cast of extras. Audience members had an image they could carry away with them.

Night after night, we create our own tableaux. In some families, the father gets served first. In others, it's the children. Many families opt for whoever sticks his fork in first.

So these rituals help us understand who is important, who gets to be fussed over, who has first choice. I grew up dreading hearing a whispered "FHB" if we had unexpected guests. *Family Hold Back* meant that those who heard the quiet warning were to take small portions, eat slowly, act as if they were full when in fact they were eyeing the morsel on the lucky guest's plate.

Not all supper rituals are fun. I have heard stories about a father who set the timer to thirty minutes; after that, all food would be taken away. One man told me that his mother set her timer to ten minutes. If you didn't finish your food in that time, you would be given another helping and would have to start eating all over again. Bad meals, bad rituals, are often about the arbitrary exercise of raw power, or the constant replaying of family rifts.

But rituals have great power for smoothing over the rough spots, helping us to regroup and heal. Because we are sharing a pleasurable sensuous experience (the only one that's public, it's been said), we reinforce pleasurable associations with family members. The rise of the hormone oxytocin after a meal is linked to feelings of calm and connection. Supper is a small daily treat we give ourselves. If we are frantically busy, it's a time to slow down. If our days are solitary and slow, a sociable meal can bring a welcome stimulus.

During summer vacations when I was a teenager, I sometimes visited the house that my grandmother shared with my aunt and uncle who had no children of their own. Grandma insisted that, even though it was fine for me to run around in shorts all day, at suppertime I had to put on a dress, because my aunt and uncle would be coming home tired, after a hard day at work, and I should greet them the proper way.

At home with my parents, no one ever said a word about shorts or dresses. A social scientist might say that my grandmother had a higher level of ritualization than my parents. She was a generation older, had grown up in a more closed world. But her rituals made the human relationships clear. She prepared a tasty dinner; I set the table as prettily as I liked. We waited while my aunt and uncle shared their nightly predinner Scotch. During the meal, my uncle would carefully tell me a joke that was often too childish for me, but I could tell he was trying, and so I would laugh. For me, those relatively formal and subdued suppers were a nice break from the hectic meals at home. I still remember the civilized quiet of those summer evenings.

Every supper is different, and every one is the same. To reach the ritual time or psychic space, we must cross some type of border, breaking away from the workaday world, then recross that border at the end. Families who aren't very religious often retain some form of grace as a way to begin. Parents who have allowed other niceties of etiquette to slide sometimes expect their children to ask to be excused from the table. And being sent away from the table remains a daunting punishment. Nobody wants to be cast out of the circle.

The culture of the family is profound in its power. Decades after the fact, we can still recite the rules, whether spelled out or implied, of our childhood meals — who sits where, what time it is eaten, who can be guaranteed to sit tight-lipped in injured silence, who will regale the assembled with his latest escapade. Can you remember what it was like eating supper at a friend's house when you were a child — how even the minuscule differences loomed large? Saying grace, or not saying it; drinking milk versus drinking soda or water or juice;

to a child, these mark the boundary between the known world and foreign shores.

Every time you encourage your toddler not to bang her spoon on the table, every time you cock your head and listen as your spouse, or your child, tells some story from the day, you are creating your family culture. You are saying, *This is who we are*: the people who, once they get old enough, do not bang their spoons on the table; the people who have things happen to them during the day, and are capable of forming their experiences into tales, and know how to listen as tablemates tell them.

When Bradd Shore was a young Peace Corps volunteer in Samoa in the 1970s, he was fascinated by the cultural differences he encountered, and by the way that different rituals spoke to similar human needs. We aren't exactly the only people who link feeding and caring. In Samoa, for example, the word for family, *aiga*, means "to eat." In Tahiti, an adopted child is sometimes called the "feeding child." Even for twenty-first-century Americans, eating from the same plate is a mark of intimacy. We may give our taboos around sharing food a veneer of concern about health, but think about how quickly we set those concerns aside for people we care about. A teenage couple sipping from the same milk shake is a cultural icon. More recently, sharing restaurant desserts has become a social norm.

So when Shore, who became an anthropologist, set up MARIAL, the Emory Center for Myth and Ritual in American Life, he understood the importance of the family meal. "It's not only a symbolic time — everyone sits down together — demonstrating the unity of the family, but it's one of the few times everyone has a chance to communicate with each other face-to-face."

Ritual provides us with a *stop-time* feeling, a time-out-of-time that is especially important in our contemporary American world. Shore remembers, "When I was a kid, generally six o'clock was dinnertime. You'd never find people scheduling meetings until seven or eight o'clock." But, he says, "family time is no longer privileged by society."

That is such an important notion, I would like to repeat it. Family time is no longer privileged by society. The world around us is saying, *Hey, if you want to count on having regular time together, sorry, you're on your own. We'll give you a couple of holidays a year, but anything more than that, and you're bucking the trend.* As recently as a generation ago in our culture, family time was sacred time, untouchable. Now we suffer from what social scientists call a time famine.

Shore says, "I think of the family meal as a victim of the extreme atomization in American life." We have always been a nation of individualists, but in the last generation our expectations for many kinds of community life — family, civic, religious — have plummeted.

Shore knows this from intimate experience. His wife spent more than three decades working as a flight attendant. Because her schedule varied from week to week, the Shores raised their children "at the edge of flextime." Shore remembers it as serial single parenthood. "We'd pass the kids off. We had fitful babysitting. We managed successfully, but with great stress, to produce a good family."

You might think that Shore, with his global worldview and his beat-the-clock parenting, would be pessimistic about maintaining the kinds of modest, home-based rituals that nourish us. "If families don't carve out a set of family rituals, there's the natural tendency of other things to take that place," he says. But he is actually very positive. His broad perspective tells him that rituals are human institutions. His own experience has shown him how they evolve and change, as well as how resilient families can be. He calls family dinner "a kind of ritual that is a very powerful option. Ritual is something that can be constructed as a family. It may appear arbitrary to the kids, but once they do it three or four times, they become quite attached to it. Ritual is a very powerful tool to use against the large-scale forces that are pulling us apart. It really is a matter that individuals can take into their own hands. It helps if workplace schedules change, but I think of it as a very life-giving area in our lives. Several nights a week, you have to make this a priority. The answer is pretty easy — just do it."

He recommends that you consult your own background, because rituals that you grew up with, or that have a historical, cultural, or religious meaning for you, will have more resonance. But you always have the option of borrowing, inventing, stealing, or combining. "In the life of kids, in the life of families, we have very short memories. If something's been done for two or three years, it's always been done." As parents, we can feel besieged by strong, seductive forces that threaten family life. But we are the authorities within our own homes.

When family therapists want a shortcut to understanding family dynamics, they will sometimes zero in on everyday rituals. They call them snapshots of how families function. They can see who's weak, who's strong, who's in, who's out; where the family lies along the rigidity–flexibility axis, the individual–group line; how much a family focuses on the "order" part of rituals, and how much on the "spontaneity" aspect. As well, therapists use ordinary rituals — and supper is the most common — to help fractured families heal.

I met a psychologist at a party who talked about a family where the mom regularly spent large amounts of time cooking elaborate suppers that her family didn't care about, which set her up for feeling resentful. Another family had "presented" with an anorexic child. When he asked them about their suppers, he discovered that this middle-class professional family didn't have any kind of table where the family could eat together. They came into the kitchen, got their food, and kept moving. The fact that the daughter — who'd grown up with no supervision or structure around food — could not regulate her eating in a reasonable way should not have come as a surprise.

At that same party, I met a woman who had two teenagers and a marriage that was coming unraveled. Her husband had recently moved out, and their daughter had decided to live with him while their son stayed with her in the "family" home. After a few months, she said, she realized that she and her son had stopped eating supper together. Each one was separately eating take-out food, standing up in the kitchen watching TV. She missed their accustomed time of connection, and she figured her son did, too. So she made a real effort to reinstate meals, just for the two of them.

"If I can't shop, I make sure that someone does," she says. "At least I come home and cook. I find, with the preparation, the eating, and the cleanup, it's two hours. Sometimes it's the best two hours of my day. It's relaxing. And for him, it means I'm around; I'm doing something. He can come in and talk to me."

On busy nights, this working mom depends on food she's cooked ahead and frozen. On weekends, she either makes whole dishes or else fries up a batch of onions or steams some vegetables, so she'll have ingredients ready during the week. She says that having real, home-cooked foods and a time to eat them together has given the new family situation a framework of dependable warmth. Reinstating an important routine is helping her and her son create a new "normal" for them both.

If we listen to the insistent blare of advertising, we are convinced that we have no time for rituals, no time for centering ourselves in company with each other. On TV, supper is often a succession of one-liners. Or a race. How little time can we spend getting food on the table? Or eating? Or being together? Better to hop into our cars and buy something else that promises to make our family time go even more quickly. Because, you know, we really have no time.

But time is the one thing we do have, no matter how rich or how poor, no matter our circumstances. Time is how we measure out our lives. It is the gift that we give others, and ourselves. We shortchange ourselves and those we love by our insistence that we have too many things to do. And so we don't allow ourselves to do the things that we can.

The Canadian sociologist Kerry J. Daly interviewed parents who had young children. They were "time starved." They were "hemorrhaging time." When Daly set up his table outside a university-run day care center to sign parents up for a study on family time, too many of them were literally running to notice that he was there. These parents were, for the most part, well aware of their problem, but instead of figuring out how to get more enjoyment from the time they did have, they were banking the present for the future, when they would be able to produce a specific type of experience that they felt would be worthy of being remembered. One father took a lot of pictures because, he said, "Someday I'll get around to living that life, or something. Living the life I missed."

Ritual helps us to get more out of our time right now. It gives us access to a more intense form of time, boiling experience down to its essence. Think about the times you have been overwhelmed by grief or by joy. Think of how you noticed the smallest gesture. This is what ritual can do: It can prepare us to be moved. So set the table, cook the food, call the kids. Light the candles, or say grace, or check on those laps and those napkins. Do whatever it is you do to begin this time apart. Now give yourself over to it. Be prepared to laugh or cajole or discuss or listen or raise your eyebrows. Be aware of the forms, and then lose yourself through them. This is your family. This is tonight.

— 3 —

How Eating Supper Makes Us Strong

BECAUSE MARSHALL DUKE is a grandfather who worries about his progeny's staying in touch with their roots, he peppers his conversation with the occasional Yiddish proverb or phrase. One of his favorites, translated, is *Whatever doesn't kill you makes you stronger.* A clinical psychologist at Emory University, Duke also worries about some of his students — the ones who are not especially strong, who don't seem too good at bouncing back, who crumble when they get a bad grade. He thinks the problem begins with the parents. His theory is that, in their desire to protect their offspring from tragedy and misery, as well as from garden-variety frustration and boredom, they may have protected them too much. So when these kids get to college and something untoward happens, they don't know how to cope.

"It's not like we're looking for tragedy," Duke says, "but bad things happen."

In recent years, psychologists have been paying increased attention to what might be called the *bad things happen* model of life. Instead of concentrating only on pathology, they are looking to understand its opposite — how some people suffer tragedy and trauma, and yet go on to do quite well. Their goal is to build this resilience into children. Or as Duke puts it, "to deal with what's in this life."

Based on his clinical work, Duke had a sense that kids who knew more about their family background tended to be more resilient. This notion that we get strength from our family ties, from our antecedents, flies in the face of our peculiarly American celebration of self-invention. It is also out of step with the way that we Americans structure our families. Because we count the family as the nuclear, child-rearing unit, we create families whose goal is to self-destruct. We define successful off-spring as those who move out and away. Extended families almost never share homes or businesses, and the leisure time we spend together is often quite limited and formal.

Duke wanted to study whether, as he suspected, a child's rootedness in his family contributed to his stability and resilience. So, along with colleagues at MARIAL, the Emory-based multidisciplinary organization that studies middle-class working families, he looked into how children learned about family lore. The study group thought about using family reunions, as well as the kinds of activities that fall under the religious, ethnic, and cultural umbrellas. But the researchers decided that the most consistent, ongoing learning about our forbears takes place — you guessed it — at the family dinner table.

Beginning in 2001, Duke and his colleagues arranged for the members of forty-two families, each of whom had a child between nine and thirteen years old, to remember and dis-cuss a negative and a positive past event, which were recorded. The families also recorded two dinnertime conver-sations. In addition, the parents were asked to tell stories about their families. But when they did, all was not sweetness and light. Duke says, "They told horrible stories about bank-ruptcies, losing jobs, having to move, accidents; one family talked about a murder."

But Duke pulls back to consider the context. "You have to look at where they're telling about it. They're in the safety of their own home. The message is: *Terrible things have happened, but we're okay, the family survives.* We're thinking it gives the kids grounding, a sense of place, a sense of context." And he goes on: "Kids find heroes in their own family." It works the other way, too. Because they are kids, "Sometimes they find one [family member] that's most annoying."

Duke knew about the nonheroic branch of his own family. "I used to have an Uncle Hershel. He was a legend in our family. Whenever anyone had a grumpy face, we'd say, Uncle Hershel's face was grumpy; his face froze."

In order to measure how much the children in the study knew about their family background, Duke's group put together what they called a Do You Know scale. This included questions like, "Do you know where some of your grandparents grew up? Do you know some of the illnesses and injuries that your parents experienced before you were born? Do you know some of the lessons that your parents learned from good or bad experiences? Do you know some jobs that your parents had when they were young?"

They ended with the legacy of Uncle Hershel. The final question, tongue in cheek, was, "Do you know anyone in your family whose face froze?" When the results were tabulated, 15 percent of the kids said they knew someone in their family whose face had frozen. College students produced similar results.

When the group wrote a working paper about their research,

they called it *Of Ketchup and Kin: Dinnertime Conversations as a Major Source of Family Knowledge, Family Adjustment, and Family Resilience.*

In addition to the Do You Know scale, the authors, whom I'll call the Ketchup Group, also measured the kids according to several standardized psychological tests. They found that the more kids knew about their families, the better they measured up. So those ridiculous stories, as well as the more serious ones, might actually have some value. As the Ketchup Group wrote, "These give-and-take interactions go beyond influencing memories for the events; they encourage perspective-taking, critical thinking, theory-building, and relationship roles within the family. . . . We propose that family narratives contribute to the current well-being and psychological immunity of its individual members."

That is, we are our stories. Hearing the family tales again and again over time anchors our sense of who we are, and gives us a feeling of belonging and hope.

The supper table is just the kind of place where this type of talk comes up naturally. A student of Duke's carried out a study that showed that kids bring up an average of six different topics per meal. That means conversations can be rich and varied. Dinner is a wonderful occasion for offhand learning because it's low-key — the opposite of quality time. Instead of saying, in effect, *Now we're going to have some meaningful interaction,* what happens is that when your child makes a joke while she's passing the ketchup, her sense of humor reminds you of Cousin Maxine. And so you tell your kid about the cousin and the connection. Or your child's miserable grumpy face allows you to bring up the story of Uncle Hershel.

This is nice for parents for a couple of reasons. It takes some of the burden off them; they can bring Uncle Hershel to the dinner table, even if he lives a thousand miles away or is no longer even walking this earth. If a child learns that a beloved, successful adult was unhappy at some point, or failed some critical test early in life, she sees that it's possible to learn from experience, to try again, and, eventually, to succeed. The dinner table conversations of my own childhood recounted daring escapes from the tsar's army, grandstanding gestures against grim poverty, and, incredibly, the admission that my successful and upstanding father had been caught by his high school principal forging fifty absence notes. ("That was when I decided I'd better get serious," he said.)

When the Ketchup Group analyzed the recordings of meals, conversations "seem to shift back and forth among food-related content, school-related content, family issues, problem-solving, and the like." Families shift effortlessly and, one assumes, unconsciously, between meatballs and myths. Food-related conversation (pass the salt) and non-food-related (what happened in school that day) showed up in a more or less one-third/two-thirds split.

The Emory team's report includes a transcript of a child talking with his parents and sibling about studying fungi in school that day. Then the dad abruptly changes the subject — "Let's talk a little bit about the Mexican Revolution" — and goes on to describe how the same wars are called by different names in different countries. (We are told that this family is of Mexican heritage.) The child asks, "Does all this have to do with my brother's report?" (the sibling is studying the Mexican Revolution in school) and the mom answers, "Uh-huh," while the father says, "No, it has to do with your general knowledge." The conversation then returns to the Mexican War of Independence against the Spaniards. The fact that one of his children is studying something related to his family's background gives the dad an opportunity to inject a bit of history from his own family's perspective. The kids expand their knowledge, learn about how different groups might approach the same historical event in different ways, and see how much their father knows and cares — both about history and about them — all while chowing down. We can picture the kids not even particularly looking at the father while he gives his little historical gloss. But it is all sinking in.

The next example is my personal favorite. It gives a sense of the glorious goofiness of eating with children. It shows how families switch gears without thinking, giving kids a free-ranging tour of the world. It shows the TC (target child) being a child; not being cooperative, then trying to engage the dad in conversation by inquiring into the parents' past, then trying to finesse a bit of food preparation while his parents both direct him and enjoy his efforts. This fleet-footed conversation is as textured as a Shakesperean play. It begins with the mother trying to get her child to converse, and with the child pointedly ignoring her efforts. Then the child says,

> TC: Love at first sight, huh?
> MOM: Yeah.
> TC: Dad? Never mind. Was it really love at
>   first sight with you two?
> MOM: Oh, please.
> TC: It was probably a divorce at one point.
>   (Snickers.)
> MOM: No.
> TC: Is this how you do it?
> MOM: Oh no, honey. First you toast it.

The conversation moves to food-preparation details that escalate to the child insisting he doesn't want cheese, and then, apparently, throwing some food.

> TC: The cheese just sort of stuck to that, I swear to God.
> MOM: You think it's gonna be love at first sight for you.
> TC: No.
> MOM: Ooh, you have ketchup on your finger.
> TC: It's gonna be kill at first sight.
> MOM: That's lovely. What's that supposed to mean?

For this family, it means cheese, laughter, and (maybe) love at first sight. But for the researchers, it meant something more. These seemingly random conversations showed a definite correlation with an extremely important measurement in social science research. It is called locus of control, and it means having a sense of the self as agent: choosing to direct your thoughts and energies toward accomplishment, and not being held back by anxiety or feelings of inadequacy. Locus of control means having a sense of power and effectiveness; of being able to exert some control over your environment.

To wrap up their findings, the Ketchup Group correlated two kinds of information: the Do You Know scale, and the children's measurement according to locus of control. (Did they have an Uncle Hershel equivalent, and did they think of themselves as being effective in the world?)

When group members linked these two variables, they found that both related directly to another extremely important concept — the child's perception of family functioning. That is, these two factors — how much a child knew about family history, and how effective the child felt in the world — were critical in whether or not the child thought his family did a good job. Kids who knew where they came from and who felt that they could exert some control over their lives had good opinions of their families.

The Ketchup Group's study assumed even more significance thanks to a quirk of timing. The baseline data had been gathered on three-quarters of the families just when 9/11 struck. A MARIAL graduate student, Amber Lazarus, realized that, sadly, the world had given them an opportunity to test their thesis about whether family knowledge helped children respond to adversity. In 2003, Lazarus was able to study twenty-one of the thirty-two families who had been part of the original 2001 study. (She referred to 2001 as Time One and 2003 as Time Two.) When she set out to reinterview twenty-one families, Lazarus says, "I was really open to what I would find."

She asked each family as a whole, and each child separately, to tell stories that were positive, and stories that were negative. The positives included things like sleep-overs and family vacations; the negatives included the death of a grandparent, and, for one child, a bout with childhood cancer. Then she asked them what they remembered about 9/11.

"The 9/11 stories varied quite a bit," she says. At the time of the attack, "Some families were very open about what they said. Some allowed the children to experience the pictures," while others did not. One mother, who was a flight attendant, even took her children on a trip to Ground Zero. At the other extreme, Lazarus says, some parents shielded their children from the event, not allowing them to see pictures of it. And of course parents varied in the types and intensity of emotions that they expressed and encouraged their children to express. "A lot of the kids remembered being taken out of school on that day. Although some were just taken to soccer practice, others stayed home with the family talking about it."

The children and parents were again given a battery of psychological tests, including the locus of control scale and the Do You Know questionnaire. Lazarus calls the results "statistically significant. Knowledge of family history accounted for approximately 36 percent of the total variance in family functioning." That means that the mere fact of knowing more about their family's history correlated extremely highly with how well children thought their families functioned. The results carried through after 9/11. "Children that actually had higher scores, knew more information about their family, were actually stronger at Time Two than kids who prior to 9/11 were more externally controlled." (Being externally controlled means they felt that external events just happened to them, and they had little power to affect their own lives.) "Kids who had higher scores rated their families as functioning better, had higher self-esteem."

Lazarus writes that, when facing the stresses of life, "the most consistent protective factor appears to be the family unit . . . adversity strengthens the family unit by igniting the possibility for personal and relational transformation and growth. . . . Knowing family history can be a protective factor in times of adversity and crisis. . . . Together, these findings suggest that family narratives have important implications for resiliency."

Twenty-one families does not constitute a huge study. But it does give some sense that simply kidding around together at the dinner table actually allows us to do serious emotional work.

ONE TRUE THING

While the Ketchup Group set its sights on supper from the get-go, a very different research group was caught by surprise when it discovered the power of family meals. The National Center on Addiction and Substance Abuse at Columbia University, known as CASA, has, as its mandate, finding ways to keep kids from destructive behaviors (the use of drugs, alcohol, and tobacco, as well as teen pregnancy). In 1996, CASA researchers ran a study to see what, if anything, differentiated the kids who engaged in these actions from those who did not. They talked to about twelve hundred teens, aged twelve to seventeen, and to an equal number of parents. They included all kinds of variables and factored out race, class, and ethnicity. The results were not what they expected at all. They found that, when it came to predicting kids' behavior, eating dinner with family was more important than church attendance, more important even than grades at school.

CASA has repeated these surveys every year since, refining the questions and focusing on different aspects of teenage behavior. And every year, eating supper together regularly as a family tops the list of variables that are within our control. Kids who eat more family dinners do better than those who eat a few. Kids who share a few dinners weekly do better than the ones who have none at all. In 2003, CASA described the case this way: "The number [of teens] who have regular family dinners drops by 50 percent as their substance abuse risk increases sevenfold."

Here are some of the results of the 2003 survey:

> Compared to teens who have family dinners twice a
> week or less, teens who have dinner with their fami-
> lies five or more nights in a week are:

- · 32 percent likelier never to have tried cigarettes.
- · 45 percent likelier never to have tried alcohol.
- · 24 percent likelier never to have smoked pot.

Those who eat lots of family dinners are almost twice as likely to get A's in school as their classmates who rarely eat as a family. Even boredom factors in. Teens who say they are bored are 50 percent more likely to smoke, drink, get drunk, and use illegal drugs. And which teens are more likely to say they are bored? Two to one, it's teens who rarely eat with their families.

CASA has also measured teen stress. Kids who have regular family meals are half as likely to be highly stressed as those who rarely have dinner. And "stressed kids are twice as likely to use drugs," according to Joseph A. Califano Jr., CASA's chairman and president, as well as a former U. S secretary of health, education, and welfare.

Califano explains why the numbers have ramifications far beyond even substance abuse: "If you look at the problems this country has — substance abuse is either causing or exacer-bating them. Eighty percent of the two million people in our prisons are there for substance abuse. If you look at the major diseases, smoking, drinking, and especially drugs have a major impact. In child abuse, 70 percent of cases involve drug- and alcohol-abusing parents. In teen pregnancy, the vast majority of one or both of the young parents were high at the time the pregnancy occurred. For AIDS, the biggest numbers of new cases involve drug users." So our need to keep our kids from substance abuse should be intense.

But here comes the troubling disconnect: Just at the time when substance abuse rises, from ages twelve to seventeen, is the time when family dinners decline. When you look at high school juniors and seniors, only a third have dinner with their parents on a regular basis. It's easy to see how this comes about. Older kids are busy, often tightly scheduled. In many ways, they are quite capable of being on their own, managing busy lives full of activities, jobs, schoolwork, and friends. It is easy to lose track of the fact that they still need the regular contact, the feeling that they are part of a group. They still need, and crave, adult guidance, even if they communicate the opposite.

The sad thing is that many parents opt out at this point, feeling there's not much they can do. More than a third of the parents in CASA's 2002 survey felt they had little influence over their teens' decisions about tobacco, drug, and alcohol use. Yet when CASA looked at the kids who had not tried marijuana, half of them credited their decision to their parents. Califano says, "If you can get a child to age twenty-one without using drugs or alcohol, he will not, by and large, use them later."

The implications could not be more clear: If we want our kids to lead healthier lives, we should eat with them more often. We should talk to them. We should not give up our close contact, or underestimate our influence. And we should not pull back as they enter their teenage years.

But what if we're looking at one of those chicken-and-egg questions? What if the "better" families are having more shared suppers just because that's the kind of thing they do? What if supper is not itself significant?

One group of public health professionals at the University of Minnesota tried to tease out some answers to these questions — to separate out "family connectedness" from the simple fact of eating family meals; to get closer to understanding whether the meal was the chicken or the egg. They interviewed almost five thousand teenagers in the Minneapolis–St. Paul schools about their eating habits, their mental state, and their use of various substances, while correlating all that with family meals. Their conclusion? "Frequency of family meals was inversely associated with tobacco, alcohol, and marijuana use; low grade point average; depressive symptoms; and suicide involvement. . . . Eating family meals may enhance the health and well-being of adolescents."

So the meals themselves are important — or at least they set the stage for the kinds of interaction we hope will happen between parents and teens. Parents are so important in their kids' lives. And supper is such an obvious place for kids to get regular access to parental presence and low-key attention. Family supper may not be a panacea, but it sure looks like a relatively painless fix.

CONTINUITY, CONTINUITY, CONTINUITY

At lots of family suppers, a bottle of beer or a glass of wine sits at the adult place. If this is just a part of the whole, it hardly registers. But in 15 percent of American families, alcohol is not an accompaniment to a meal, but *the* ingredient that defines the gathering. The drink, and the behavior patterns that coalesce around the drinking, form the structure of family life. The effects, which are profoundly destructive, can actually be worse for the family members than for the alcoholic. Even more troubling: Family patterns defined by alcoholism can be handed down for generations.

So, you might ask: *If we're not alcoholics, why should we care?* The answer lies in the power of ritual, especially rituals such as supper, which can help kids and families to be more resilient, to more effectively handle life's vicissitudes. The alcohol–supper matrix, in particular, can help us understand how relatively small changes can have a significant impact on family life, making room for "normalcy" in a distressing situation. In addition, these particular studies have had profound consequences for the ways that therapists think about how families function.

The relation between supper and alcoholism first came to light two decades ago, thanks to a set of studies by the Center for Family Research at George Washington University. In 1987, psychiatrist Peter Steinglass published a book with his colleagues, Linda Bennett, an anthropologist, and Steven M. Wolin and David Reiss, both psychiatrists, called *The Alcoholic Family*. The book reported on a ten-year study involving more than 150 families by researchers who wanted to know if they could break the cycle of alcoholism.

They had been refining their approach since in the late 1970s, when they had read two unrelated studies — one in London, and one in Hawaii — about resilient children. The researchers went beyond documenting the negative factors, or stressors, for children with difficult lives. Instead, they tried to puzzle out why some children emerged happy and productive despite growing up in daunting situations. The George Washington team decided to expand the concept to see if there were factors that could protect not just individual children, but entire families.

One of the researchers, Steven Wolin, had been interviewing people in alcoholic families. (These were defined as families whose self-definition was determined by the alcohol use of one or more members.) He was hearing that, during periods of heavy drinking, rituals like family supper that had been important to the family tended to disappear. He decided to turn that fact around, to look at it in a positive way: If some alcoholic families were able to maintain their rituals (and supper was a primary one), did this bode well for family strength? Would the children of alcoholics be less likely to become alcoholic themselves if their families were able continue to do "normal" things, such as eating supper together?

The team interviewed more than 150 families about alcohol use spanning three generations. They wanted to know why some children of alcoholics fell into relationships defined by alcohol use (either their own or a spouse's), while others were able to break the pattern. It's worth mentioning here that even nondrinking families can create their identity around alcohol: the folks who haunt self-help meetings, or insist that they never ever touch a drop.

In the book, Steinglass and his team make a distinction between a family who has an alcoholic member and something he calls an Alcoholic Family: a family who defines itself around alcohol. His line for separating the two is whether or not the alcohol-related behavior affects family rituals. And the ritual he most often uses for illustration is family supper.

In one family, on the weekends that the father spends drinking, joint meals are suspended and family members retreat to their own corners. In another, the drinking is constant. ("Ed stands in the corner of the dining room with a drink in his hand while the rest of us eat. We're afraid to say anything that might set him off.") In some families, dinner doesn't happen because the children are off tracking down their father at the neighborhood bars, or because Mom, the family drinker and homemaker, can't manage to produce a meal.

In those types of situations, the family's "mission" changes, because it must focus an inordinate amount of its energy on maintaining the status quo; on "managing" the alcoholic. Consequently, much of the other "work" of the family — nurturing children, helping individual growth, easing relationships with the outside world — remains undone. The family is brittle, its mission stalled.

Supper is an important way of understanding and changing this dynamic. In *The Alcoholic Family*, the authors liken family rituals to "condensed, prepackaged training modules intended to convey to all family members the important facts about family identity." From the family's point of view, rituals "might be a vehicle for the transmission of important shared beliefs and values (including those surrounding alcohol use and alcohol-related behavior) to the next generation." From the researchers' viewpoint, "no other family regulatory behavior is so clearly reflective of underlying identity issues as is family ritual behavior." Condensed in form and richly symbolic, it helps researchers and clinicians get a "snapshot" of a family.

In the contest between the alcoholic and a family ritual such as supper, the alcoholic rarely accommodates to the family event; it is the event that must be adjusted or even transformed if the alcoholic family member is to be included. Supper then becomes a trigger for a family to express some emotion that is otherwise held under wraps. And it bears repeating that the ensuing behavioral changes are often worse for the nondrinking family members than for those who actually imbibe. So we can see how supper would get fused with alcoholic identity. *Because my dad likes his beer, at supper we always . . . Once my wife starts drinking before dinner, we never . . .*

According to Steinglass, rituals are important because they are ubiquitous, they contain "the myths, history, and identity of the family," they are conscious activities, and they "can be taught to families who don't have them, changed in families who are so inclined, and dropped in families who collectively make such decisions." They are critically important, and they are under our control. Rituals like supper are where family identity happens, and where it can change, for good or for ill.

It stands to reason that in families who are able to maintain their rituals, children have a better chance of constructing a self-image around other issues. (*My dad may drink, but he manages to make it to the table. He may not eat, but he tries to listen to us.*) In some families, rituals are kept alive through creative evasion. (*I feed you kids early because, by the time your dad gets home, he will be too tired.*) But families whose rituals are "invaded" by alcoholic behaviors will more likely to produce children whose identities are forever influenced by liquor, like the family whose mealtimes ceased when Dad was drinking. If your childhood was marked by suppers in which people ate and talked in a convivial way, you will probably reproduce those kinds of meals as an adult. But if your association with "supper" is "Mom's belittling us kids" or "Dad's throwing a fit" or "no supper at all," you will have much less to work with. (We might make a similar case for families mobilized around a member with a serious mental or physical disease.)

There is, however, an upside to all of this. The team found that, no matter what a person's background, he could improve his own family by being deliberate about family rituals. Now, on the surface, that sounds obvious: If you don't want to be a drunk, don't spend your suppertime drinking. But it goes much deeper. Being involved with alcohol doesn't only mean drinking. It can mean living with an alcoholic partner. It can mean allowing alcohol to be a central organizing principle of your family's life. Even if you spend all your spare time going to AA meetings, if all your social life revolves around never touching a drop, your life is still controlled by the bottle.

So if the goal is to relegate alcohol to a place where it's not basic to family functioning, it's helpful to take the long, long view:

Like people, families have life cycles. They are formed, they expand, they mature, they contract, and they die. And they leave legacies to the next generation. In the early days, when a couple becomes "a couple," whether by moving in together or through marriage, one of their most important issues is establishing boundaries. The new unit must define who is inside the family circle (possibilities include siblings, parents, step-relations, favorite aunts, family friends), what kinds of contact they will have with their families of origin (drop in anytime; maintain a regular schedule; see each other only at formal group occasions), whether they will favor the heritage of one family over another, and how deliberate they will be about all of the above.

You can see how the alcohol scenario might play out here. One young woman, the daughter of an alcoholic father, might find herself, almost without noticing, in a relationship with a boyfriend who drinks his way through his evenings, becoming more abusive the more he drinks. Another alcoholic's daughter might bond strongly with her new, nonalcoholic in-laws, carefully emulating their habits and customs, distancing herself from her family of origin.

Over time, as families expand, adding children to their home, they establish their family values, priorities, and style. This is when a family benefits from consistency and stability, so that family members are free to use their energy to work and grow in the outside world.

The alcoholic family, however, is working hard just to maintain its equilibrium. Because alcohol-fueled behaviors can be so disruptive, alcoholic families focus on a type of rigid stability that comes at a huge price. Alcohol often masks other family dynamics or individual needs, but it becomes part of a dependable, if unsatisfying, cycle of family relationships. And the cycle's very predictability makes it difficult to change.

Then, as the family enters its late stage, as children move away and the family unit contracts, it passes its legacy along to the next generation. Whether they drink to excess or scrupulously avoid imbibing, alcohol is a central theme of family life.

Steinglass's studies found that alcoholic families who were able to maintain key family rituals (with dinnertime first among them) had fewer members of the next generation becoming alcoholic themselves. Dinnertime didn't have to be perfect; it was a positive influence just by being there. This is both common sense and an illustration of the profound ways that rituals enter our bones. It is also where the implications go far beyond alcoholic families.

When researchers talked to alcoholic families about their general functioning, some could not see how alcohol use affected them. However, as soon as the discussion turned to family rituals, everyone could understand. Steinglass talks about a sixtieth birthday party where the family made sure that the "birthday boy" always had a bottle of liquor within easy reach. The activity of the party consisted entirely of drinking. When the man's teenage son, upset by the spectacle, attempted to remove the bottle, his wife made him put it back. We can imagine that the boy carried an image of that event for a long time.

"Rituals are, above all else, memorable," Steinglass writes. "Though each nuclear family creates its own celebrations, traditions, and patterned routines, frequently they contain elements of rituals performed in previous generations. By the same token, the rituals of the present will persist in some form into the future." Our parents live on through us, and we live through our children, not only in the sterling words of advice we might on occasion offer, but also in the habits of our daily lives.

This systematic way of looking at families' self-definition — their weaknesses and strengths — has many ramifications. One of the study's authors, Steven Wolin, went on to found Project Resilience, a strengths-based approach that breaks down resilience into teachable parts.

Steinglass has become executive director of the Ackerman Institute, a pioneering center for family therapy based in New York City. When I visit him, he talks to me about a field called family resilience — which, he says, marks a very important shift in direction. "Most of American medicine, American psychiatry, is pathology oriented." It's much more important, he says, especially when you're managing chronic conditions, to focus on how families solve problems. "This approach fits in with public health, with a family systems mode." By harnessing a family's strengths the therapist can be much more effective at helping the family work out solutions.

He gives me an example: a group of families who have been meeting at the institute, all of whom have a family member with cancer. One of the devices they've used is to have each family create a family motto, a bumper sticker, a brief description of what their family stands for.

Then, Steinglass reports, he asks the group, "To what extent does that motto have to do with cancer? Do you tell cancer it has to play by the family's rules, or have you given in to the cancer?"

On the face of it, that's an absurd question, and Steinglass freely admits that a surgeon would think he was nuts. But he continues, telling me that he asks the group of families, "Would it be possible to decide that dinnertime will be cancer-free time?" Families who are able to do this can usually find a place for the illness in their life while keeping it in its place. "It gives you a sense you're in charge rather than the cancer's in charge, and that it's legitimate to think about those things." This harks back to the concept of locus of control we learned from the Ketchup Group.

Taking constructive family actions is infinitely easier if you are regularly having family supper. Steinglass says, "If we have that vehicle [supper], it's built into our life, it's there. If you have to call a special meeting, it's much less likely it will happen. The analogy: In business, there are ongoing meetings; there are others scheduled for specific purposes." So maybe the "normal" stresses and tragedies of life — death, divorce, chronic illness — can be mitigated if we have the support of meaningful rhythms in our days. If we know we can count on regular family contact, we are more apt to be effective as a family. As individuals, we contribute to our family. But the collective strength of the family helps us as well.

For another example of the interplay between daily family rituals and "normal" problems, let's take a quick look at asthma. In 2000, a Syracuse University study included eighty-six families, half of whom had children with asthma. They found that family routines and family rituals correlated strongly with lower levels of anxiety. And anxiety is linked to asthma. Again, when the social scientists listed family rituals, dinner was the number one.

In the case of asthma, there are specific outcomes that are directly linked to anxiety: number of school days missed, number of hospitalizations and emergency room visits, amount of mechanical ventilation. So this moves beyond the family to become an issue of medical expenditures and public health.

Here's what the study concluded: "Under conditions of multiple stressors, family rituals may offer one avenue for families to stabilize their lives and provide a sense of belonging." So eating together may help us relax enough to breathe more easily.

And here is one final study. In 1995 and 1996, the National Longitudinal Study of Adolescent Health interviewed ninety thousand teenagers and twenty thousand parents. This study was carried out by the National Institute of Child Health and Human Development, a part of the National Institutes of Health, and was mandated by Congress. Although it will take a decade to tabulate the results, the first report, published in 1997, was titled *Connections That Make a Difference in the Lives of Youth*. The conclusion?

> Time and time again, the home environment emerges as central in shaping health outcomes for American youth. Controlling for the number of parents in a household, controlling for whether families are rich or poor, controlling for race and ethnicity, children who report feeling connected to a parent are pro-

tected against many different kinds of health risks, including: emotional distress and suicidal thoughts and attempts; cigarette, alcohol, and marijuana use; violent behavior; and early sexual activity.

When a parent is physically present in the home at key times, and has high expectations for the child's education, children are on the road to being protected from involvement in behaviors that can damage them. . . .

Adolescents are also protected from emotional distress by: their parents being present at key times during the day (in the morning, after school, at dinner, and at bedtime). . . . When a parent is physically present in the home at key times, youth are less likely to use cigarettes, alcohol, and marijuana, and less likely to be emotionally distressed.

So we can see how it makes sense to continue meaningful family rituals through good times and bad. Still, when I am speaking to Steinglass, I must ask him the cause-or-effect question. Or, to use social science speak: Is supper a marker or a mechanism? Are families who communicate with and support each other more likely to eat supper together, or does eating supper make families function better?

Steinglass answers my question with a question: "Are you making this easier for yourself or harder for yourself?" Why not structure family life so that it's likely to work better? Why not build in supports that can help families every day?

We have ways of looking at families that make sense (families as interrelated systems; families as units that change over time). We have access to institutions (regular family rituals, specifically supper) that work in powerful ways. Why shoot ourselves in the foot, he is saying. Why not use what we have when we're looking for instruments of positive continuity, positive change?

EATING AND ORDER

Is it possible for a whole society to be eating-disordered? It's certainly beginning to look that way. The anxiety that a previous generation lavished on right behavior has morphed into anxiety about right food choice. We have become food phobics, food obsessives, food worshipers, parsing our unprecedented bounty into categories that give us some sense of control. *Bad person to eat fried food. Slacker to have gained that extra weight. Uncaring parent to feed your kids chemicals. Uptightnik to care so much about it all.* Naturally, the supper table is where this all plays out.

We eat oddly, buffeted by idiosyncratic whims, informed by what one nutritionist calls "the health terrorist message of the day." We are too busy to prepare meals, too pressured by competing claims of taste, nutrition, convenience, and fashion to rationally consider what we eat. We have no idea what standards to apply. And when we eat alone, we have no one casting a caring eye on what, or how much, we put into our mouths.

Here are some of the friends and family who have come to my house recently for dinner: an ethical vegetarian, a worried-about-body-odors vegetarian, a worried-about-weight-control vegetarian, people who are kosher, people who are partially kosher, an anorexic, a person who is medically obese who eats as much as possible, some who say they only eat protein but make up for it with dessert, some who really do try to only eat protein, fat phobics, carbohydrate avoiders, one person who swears by whichever diet gets the nod from the health section of the *New York Times*, any number who try to eat only a minimum of red meat, a few fans of unrefined foods and fiber, one diabetic, and one who, when she was battling cancer, went macrobiotic. And those are just the adults. No wonder many people throw up their hands and let the whole meal business slide.

But here is the problem: When we don't eat regular, social meals, we pull the nutritional rug out from underneath us. If we diet, graze, or grab what we can, we lose the ability to understand what constitutes a meal, which does not necessarily mean overcooked meat, potato, and two veg, but rather some combination of nutrients, food groups, colors, flavors, and textures that presents an inviting, tasty, nutritious, and reasonably sized whole. A meal is something that is worth being hungry for; something that will satisfy us so that we will not be looking for something more an hour down the road; something that makes sense in terms of our daily, and long-term, bodily needs.

The dieticians' mantra, *Eat when you're hungry, stop when you're sated*, works best in a context of regular, nutritionally dense meals. (I would humbly amend that to nutritionally reasonable meals. To me, the concept of *nutritionally dense* is fine, as long as it leaves room for dessert.) Our bodies crave replenishment at regular intervals, and digestion takes a set amount of time. Our psyches need to connect to our fellows as well. Combining our needs for food and for sociability on some sort of regular, dependable schedule should be a no-brainer. But fewer and fewer of us do it.

At the same time, we are becoming more aware of the tragic toll of eating disorders. (A note on nomenclature: Although obesity is actually categorized as an eating disorder, in common parlance eating disorders include only anorexia and bulimia.) But health professionals stress that full-blown, life-threatening anorexia, bulimia, and what physicians call "morbid obesity" represent only the extremes of disordered eating. As we lose our consensus over what, and how, we should eat, we encourage more idiosyncratic and just plain weird eating habits. Our food court world, where everything is available all the time, means never having to compromise. Our glorification of individuality elevates caprice to the level of dogma. While we monitor which celebrities are checking into treatment for diagnosed eating disorders, garden-variety dysfunctional eating is so common, it hardly registers.

One therapist tells me about a client of hers who struggles with bulimia. The fact that this woman's mother was a caterer with a home-based business makes her story a bit more dramatic than most, but it's a good metaphor. Picture her childhood home overflowing with wonderful foods, and with little or no structure. There were no family meals, no sitting down together at regular times with other people. The woman never learned what constituted a "normal" portion, a reasonable eating schedule, or an appropriate combination of foods. She had access to a continuous feast, but little guidance about how to use it.

Now, as an adult, she knows that she should eat meals, but she can't seem to get herself on a schedule. To keep her weight under control, she will skip a meal, then let herself get so ravenous that she will wolf down a huge amount, which makes her feel guilty, and so she responds by making herself vomit. She is trapped in a cycle of reward, guilt, and punishment. Food is not pleasurable and nourishing; it's a torment.

We are fast approaching a tipping point on the disordered-eating scale. We can't assume that, at the end of the day, adults will sit down with children and model what it means to eat a more or less balanced meal. We cannot assume that adults will know how to cook. One researcher points out that *cooking*, for many of us, has come to mean "warming."

Out in the world, we drive past food offering after food offering after food offering. At home, the TV urges us to eat, eat, eat; it advertises concoctions that nutritionists call food porn, interspersed with too-good-to-be-true diet plans. It's hard to find anyplace where large quantities of cheap food aren't instantly available.

Like us, our children get their guidance from the media: Hate your body, try this week's diet, buy that snack food, grab it and go. In our schools, both physical education and home economics classes have been booted out or drastically reduced, while fast foods, junk foods, candy, and soda have been welcomed in. This has been done in the name of budgetary efficiency. However, in those pioneering school districts where lunchroom management has been handed over to people who care about good food served in a humane setting, the kids are happily eating baked chicken legs, wraps, chili, and couscous (part of the grain-of-the-month curriculum in the Hopkins, Minnesota, public schools), and the cafeterias are staying on budget.

Meanwhile, at home, kids learn from what we do. If we skip meals; if we move from diet to diet; if we eat standing up, grabbing a snack in front of the fridge; if we chow down mindlessly in front of the TV; if we don't eat all day and then gorge all evening; if we have categories of food that are evil, and if those evil foods are a temptation and eating them is a sin, our offspring will learn their lessons well. We shouldn't be surprised when young children assume that dieting is normal. Like us, they set up arbitrary systems that run on guilt, and that must be replaced by new systems when they realize that the current ones don't work.

According to Anorexia Nervosa and Related Eating Disorders (ANRED), a nonprofit organization, 1 percent of female adolescents suffer from anorexia, and 4 percent of college-age women from bulimia. Although their causes are varied, full-blown disorders, which may or may not be symptoms of deeper disturbances, take on a life of their own. The thinking now is that there is a genetic predisposition to the disorder, and that a wide variety of familial and personal issues can set them off.

But let's keep in mind that the obsession they set off is dieting. Dieting maintains the cycle, keeping the switch on. Experts talk about personality types, family dynamics, and triggering events, but keep returning to our cultural obsession with thinness, our assumption that food is scary, dangerous, or bad. When the Web site of the Eating Disorders Institute of Methodist Hospital in St. Louis Park, Minnesota, lists signs of eating disorders, number one is people who "eliminate entire food groups from daily intake," a definition that would include large swaths of our population. So it makes sense to visit those who treat the most damaged victims of our dieting mania if we want to learn how to establish and maintain a healthy atmosphere at home. (Bonus points: What daily habit do you think is going to turn out to be indispensable?)

On the outpatient unit of the Eating Disorders Institute,

Tuesday is Family and Friends night, the time when the ten or so clients invite people close to them to a shared meal. It's almost a rehearsal for a more "normal" family supper. In the afternoon, the group decides on the menu: It has to include a protein, two carbohydrates, a vegetable, a fat, and a dessert. (The day that I speak to them, they are planning on shrimp tortellini in cream sauce.) They shop and cook as a group, then eat all together: clients, guests, and staff. Everyone is expected to eat the same-sized portions of the same things. A staff member reminds guests there's to be no talk of food, diet, or exercise, except for something along the lines of *This tastes good* or *You guys did a good job*.

Greg Fedio, the dietician who coordinates the program, says it's amazing how often the guests forget. "So many people have food obsessions, disordered eating." In middle-class America, after sharing a good meal, a remark like *Now I'll have to exercise to work this off* is knee-jerk.

The Eating Disorders Institute also has an inpatient unit, which primarily serves adolescents. Part of this treatment is a family meal, ordered from the central kitchen. Although the whole family is strongly advised to come, many families can't manage full attendance, for all the regular reasons. But dietician Betsy Christopherson says that she pushes back at them, saying, "We have somebody hospitalized here." They are not a group of unrelated roommates. They are a family.

These hospital dinners may be the first meal the family has shared for a long time. "Or Mom might be making one thing for the patient with the eating disorder and something else for the rest of the family," Christopherson says. It is one response to a very stressful type of family meal.

In the hospital, the staff try to defuse the situation, model how to have conversations as a group, talk about something other than food, and, by example, show what normal eating looks like. "Sometimes people just have odd habits as a family," Christopherson says. "People take what they want from the freezer and then eat individually on trays in front of the TV, or in their rooms." And for many of their bulimic patients, "Life is not very structured and scheduled. Everyone's flying off in all directions. It's chaotic." Family meals can be punctuated by fighting.

When the clients return home, staff members report that, for the most part, the parents are anxious to make changes. The staff give them the same advice they would give to families without eating disorders: Have regular meals. Make it a pleasant occasion. This is not the time for corrections. Even if you're getting take-out food, sit down together. Most important: Do not engage in power struggles. If you do, you have already lost.

"I think most kids really like eating family meals, even if they gripe and complain," says Lee. "Even if it's just a few of you that can sit down together, that counts. These parents that have to work such long hours should consider making those evenings sacred. In ten years, the children will be gone. Who cares if you worked more then?"

Julie Mowery, a dietician who conducts parent education groups at the Eating Disorders Institute, takes it one step farther. She tells parents to create an environment that's not only secure, but also pleasant: "not tense, not angry. I tell people, Set a really nice table. The other thing I tell them about is taking time" — time to talk to their children, time to listen.

Still, Christopherson reminds us that, for families who aren't accustomed to having regular meals, change can be hard. "If, for fifteen years, everyone's been doing their own thing, and all of a sudden we change all the rules, it's a tough time. What it takes is parents sticking to it."

Mowery points out that all the normal problems are exacerbated for single moms. Since they have to shoulder so much responsibility with so little backup, supper is often a casualty. She tries to help them understand how important it is. For families who typically get their supper at the drive-thru window and then eat in their car, she urges them to take the extra twenty minutes and sit down inside.

Mowery treats people of all ages. And she always asks them what supper was like when they were children. "I truly have had people who said, 'We never had a family meal.'" For those folks, if they're in their twenties and thirties, dinner might have consisted of eating chips and cheese sauce out of a jar. She notes that, in general, people who are in their forties or older had family meals growing up but, if they have eating problems now, their childhood suppers were likely to have been unpleasant affairs. She gives the example of one patient who experienced "such disorder in the family, anger and fighting, she ran away from it. Her anorexia started with that. She would do anything to avoid eating."

Even more basic than setting the tone is setting the time. "One of our strategies, for both anorexia and bulimia, is to set up structured and set mealtimes and distinct snack times. It helps normalize the digestion, the satiety. I always show my patients a graph: Our bodies are made to be hungry every three to four hours. Before breakfast, and in the afternoon, there's also a little hunger blip." She says it makes sense to time our eating to correlate with our body's cycle. Fedio, one of the staff members, tells me how much he's appreciated the enforced regular eating of his current job. Before working at the clinic, he was a graduate student; his eating had been catch-as-catch-can. Now that his mealtime is regulated, he says, "Your body really appreciates it. We eat at noon for lunch, at five for dinner. On the weekends, my body says, *It's noon!*"

Mowery argues that, in the present generation, normal eating has largely been lost. She contrasts that with Europe, where her sister lives. "The Europeans will eat cheese, which has fat, and bread, which has carbohydrates," two current no-nos for Americans. But she calls their meals "very balanced. They always have fruit, and they always have vegetables. They always have dessert, but their portions are much more reasonable. We have created so much fear through the media. We sensationalize food."

Mowry says that Europeans are more likely to honor food, to eat slowly, and to savor the food and the company. She explains that there is also a biological reason to slow down. It takes fifteen to twenty minutes for the brain to register satiety. If you eat slowly, she says, "the brain and the stomach catch up with one another." That is why, if you relax and carry on a conversation while you are eating, you will have time to notice when you are actually full. People who skip meals, then wait until they are starving to eat, are more likely to down large amounts of food without tasting it, without enjoying it, without knowing when they have actually had enough.

Anorexics will typically not allow themselves to enjoy food. Bulimics will typically eat so fast and so much they are unaware of what they are consuming. Even for those of us who are "normal," those two approaches are all too recognizable.

So Mowery finds herself teaching families to enjoy their food. "Even when families travel, I say, Stop the car. Get out and make it a meal. Savor the taste." She is also a proponent of the No Bad Food school. I personally have a problem with that one. How about real junk food, I ask her. How about the stuff with zero nutritional value? I am thinking of things like chips, which don't appeal to me. I am not thinking of cookies and candies, which are equally dubious, but which I enjoy.

She gently but firmly pooh-poohs me. "The theory is, when you deprive yourself of any food, it's going to set you up to want to binge on that. Sometimes I call it the Adam and Eve syndrome. There was only one thing they couldn't have; they could have had the entire world. So what did Adam want?"

All right; I get her drift.

Of course there is no guarantee that if you maintain regular meals, you will eradicate eating disorders. But it does suggest that the absence of regular meals makes it easier for all sorts of disordered eating to thrive.

The regular-meals model can help in the fight against obesity as well. If eating is seen as a social activity that happens at specific times in a specific setting, we are less likely to overeat. We reduce the cues about when, where, and under what circumstances it is appropriate to eat. If we are served a reasonable portion, along with everyone else in the family, we learn what a moderate helping is. If we talk while we eat, if we enjoy being together, we are less likely to eat as much as we can, as fast as we can.

Thirty years ago, my friend Larry, then a psychology graduate student, worked on a very basic eating experiment. Larry invited students to come, one by one, to take a test about perception. In the course of the testing he would, offhandedly, offer a cracker from a plate on his desk. (As I recall, it was a saltine; food expectations were modest.) Some people took one of Larry's crackers, some didn't. They didn't realize it, but that cracker decision constituted the actual test. As they entered the room, Larry had surreptitiously rated the subjects as being fat or thin. The thin ones, it turned out, tended to take a cracker if it was within an hour of mealtime; the heavier ones were more likely to eat the proffered cracker no matter what time it was.

This seems to be commonsensical: Yes, the thinner people will eat less. But the important thing is that the thinner people were more likely to limit their eating to mealtimes.

Recently Jane Brody, author of the "Personal Health" column in the *New York Times*, wrote about her experience with something called Night Eating Syndrome. As a young woman far from home with a demanding job, she found herself eating nothing all day, and then eating steadily all evening. She soon gained forty pounds. After a bit of therapy, a move, and a new job, she made a decision: "If I was going to be fat, at least let me be healthy. Hungry or not, I made myself eat three wholesome meals a day, with prearranged snacks if needed and one small 'no-no' to keep me from feeling deprived." Within a month, she had lost ten pounds; within two years, she dropped another twenty-five.

So having regular, sociable suppers looks like an important tool in the fight against a spectrum of eating disorders. It teaches our bodies when to get hungry. It helps us learn when we are full. Dieticians repeatedly tell parents that the best thing they can do for their kids is to model healthy eating themselves. Have regular, pleasant, enjoyable mealtimes. Serve a variety of foods. Don't diet. Don't demonize any foods. Don't make disparaging remarks about how people look. Make sure your children know they are valued not for how they look, but for who they are.

There are no guarantees in this life, especially when it comes to raising children. But providing a healthy, calm, enjoyable environment around regular meals is a reasonable effort that can have outsized results.

— 4 —

Who, What, Where

MORE THAN TWO thousand years ago, the Greek philosopher Epicurus wrote, "We should look for someone to eat and drink with before looking for something to eat and drink, for dining alone is leading the life of a lion or wolf."

We humans are surely social animals, and much of our learning consists of watching others. Mealtimes are prime occasions for learning behaviors, skills, attitudes, and ideas. In the same way that we learn to speak, we pick up our cues about food by imitation. This is one of the most basic functions of the supper table — giving children an opportunity to see what the adults in their family, in their class, in their culture, think is good to ingest. For example, when people first become vegetarian, it takes them a while to stop looking to replace the "meat" course if they have always lived with meat at the center of the plate. I have known Russians who, when faced with a meal without potatoes, become quiet and sad. We have very specific ideas about what is good to eat. But we are not born that way.

Although baby humans come equipped with a couple of preferences — *for* sweet and *against* bitter — our species exhibits two warring food drives. We have a desire to try some new things (it might, after all, be nutritious or tasty), as well as a reluctance to put strange or unproven things into our mouths (they might make us sick). This "omnivore's dilemma" makes sense if we think of our evolutionary heritage. We need to eat a variety of foods, but we must learn to distinguish between those that are good for us and those that can harm us. We need someone to point out the poisonous mushroom as well as the tasty young fern.

Nowadays, our corner of the species has more than enough food, but we still carry the *should I—shouldn't I* question in our genes. Babies will consider a new food, trying it out in their hands, then examining it in their mouths. Sometimes they will swallow, sometimes spit it out. Accepting something new can take a long time.

Paul Rozin, a psychologist at the University of Pennsylvania who has spent decades studying food prejudices and preferences, says that we are pretty much the only animals who develop a taste for ingesting things that are, at first, unpleasant. He includes coffee, the irritant spices, and various forms of alcohol in this category.

In order to study how we acquire our likes and dislikes, Rozin and his colleagues decided to go with insects. Although many cultures eat them, Americans find them abhorrent. So Rozin bought a bunch of brand-new fly swatters: plastic objects that had never gone near a fly. They set out a variety of tasty hot soups and invited college students to be the subjects of an experiment. When presented with a soup that they liked, the students would not touch it if it had been stirred with a *brand-new* fly swatter — a clean piece of plastic just purchased from the store, unused.

In the late 1970s, Rozin accompanied an anthropologist

colleague to a small village in Mexico, near Oaxaca, where he could study food preferences by concentrating on chili peppers, those fireballs that, he says, produce oral pain and, "at moderately high levels, induce defensive reflexes, including salivation, running of the nose, and tearing of the eyes." So why on earth would anyone eat them? Chili peppers happen to be good for us, with extremely high levels of vitamins A and C. But scientists have not been able to prove that people come to like foods because of their nutritional benefit. (Any parent could have told them that.) Rozin says that the peppers, with "the saliva and the pepper flavor and burn," give some flavor to an otherwise bland and monotonous diet, which probably explains much of their appeal. But they are definitely an acquired taste.

He told the adults in the village about his interest in chili peppers. They agreed that small children didn't like them, but that, sometime around age five or six, they seemed to change their minds.

Then Rozin began his experiment. He tells me, "I tested the kids, gave them snacks that were hot and some that were not. Around the age of five or six they started preferring the hot one, just like the people said." Rozin observed that, during family meals, the children are gradually given increasing amounts of chili, although they are allowed to refuse it. "They are not rewarded in any obvious way for eating it; rather they observe that it is enjoyed by their elders. They were very non-confrontational, very relaxed. By age five to eight, most children in the village were voluntarily adding piquancy to their foods; they had come to like the 'hot' stuff after months to years of exposure to it in a natural family setting."

In the interests of science, Rozin extended his study to

include the local dogs; the villagers thought that was a riot. He offered the dogs tortillas with and without hot sauce. They invariably chose the tortillas without.

Rozin explains that, in a third-world country such as Mexico, dogs are not treated as pets; they are fed garbage. The only dog he found who liked hot sauce was one who belonged to his graduate student, and who, like a good American pet, sat next to the table during meals. "She had a social link with humans," Rozin explains. He did hear of "a few cases of chili-liking in animals . . . however, in all such cases, the animals (chimpanzees, dogs, macaque monkeys) were adored pets in homes where chili pepper was a frequent part of the diet. Perhaps these personal domesticates participated in the human social matrix that may be so important in the reversing of aversions and development of likings."

Rozin mentions the fact that, although food preferences are passed down within a culture, individual preferences are not. Parents' particular likes and dislikes seem to have little effect on their children. If everyone in my culture eats lots of meat, then my child will also. But she will not necessarily share my preference for lamb over beef. "What does get passed on is general attitudes toward food, like trying new foods or being interested in trying new foods."

Rozin thinks that, in general, American families are much too worried about food likes and dislikes. By paying so much attention to what their children are eating, they take the joy out of mealtimes. He contrasts it with Italians, where "everyone is just smiling and enjoying themselves. There's no bargaining over what gets eaten. Dessert isn't the big event."

Nutritionists say that, by telling our children they have to eat their vegetables before they can have dessert, we are teaching them two things: first, that vegetables are not nearly as good as dessert. And second, that mealtimes are the occasions for arguments, or at least for making deals.

So we are extremely susceptible to social influence when choosing what we eat. As early as the 1930s, marketers found that kids would eat foods linked with a hero, something they called the Popeye effect. The food that Mommy makes is better than the same food cooked by a stranger. When we are sick, and so returned to a more primitive, helpless state, we want the bland comfort foods of our childhood. (Doesn't everyone have a favorite "sick" food?) And think about breakfast. When we stumble into the kitchen, rubbing our eyes, we want No Surprises. We want Familiar and Plain. As the day goes on, we may get more adventurous. But so close to sleep, we want what we know.

In many cultures, food has a moral component. The Hua of Papua, New Guinea, say that a person's character is improved by eating food procured or prepared by people close to them. They encourage the appropriate relative to spit into food, to ensure that the strength of the provider is passed on. Think of how common it is, around the world, to welcome guests by offering food; how impolite it is to refuse. We come together in order to share food. And that experience strengthens our ties.

What are we to make, then, of our contemporary deification of personal preference? The food court, where everyone gets to have his own, is typically American. At home, we may offer a child broccoli once or twice, but if it is refused, we say that the child *does not eat broccoli*. But nutritionists tell us that humans are extremely conservative about trying new foods; a child can be expected to taste something ten, fifteen, or twenty times before she decides that she likes it. She may, at first, just get used to the feel of it in her mouth before spitting it out. Think of the Mexican children learning to eat chili. Even though everyone else is eating it, it still takes years for them to develop a taste for it.

At the table, children also learn how much to eat. They see what size portion they are given. They know whether or not they are expected to finish, whether they should expect seconds or thirds, whether they will be praised for eating a little or a lot. They are also aware of how much the others at the table are eating.

Thirty years after his research in Mexico, Rozin continues to examine cultural differences around food. In 2003, he published a study comparing portion size in Philadelphia and in Paris, targeting fast-food restaurants that serve the same foods in both countries.

But if the food is the same, the amounts are quite different. A medium order of fries at the Philadelphia McDonald's is a third larger than a comparable order in Paris. A scoop of Häagen-Dazs is almost twice as big on our side of the Atlantic, while a slice of Pizza Hut in Philadelphia outweighs the Paris version by almost a third. Interestingly, the French also eat more slowly, with the average Parisian spending twenty-two minutes at McDonald's while in Pennsylvania the comparable time is eight minutes less. So my memories of smaller, more leisurely meals in France a generation ago have now been measured and codified.

Just as children learn to speak by listening to the adults and children around them, they learn to eat by looking across the table. If there *is* someone sitting across the table. That socializing influence around food is one of the benefits of having family suppers. Over time, in a sociable situation, children learn to eat more challenging foods. They learn that a variety of foods can be pleasing, that the adults in their lives have expectations for them as eaters. Just as we assume that one day they will learn to brush their own teeth, or learn to drive, we assume that their tastes will broaden, and that they will eat chili peppers if they are Mexican, curry if they are Indian, paprika if they are Hungarian, and all of the above if they live in a family where a variety of food is available, and where eating is seen as an adventure. Otherwise, they will continue to eat at the level of children, keeping their food bland and sweet. It is no accident that fast foods cater to this limited, lowest-common-denominator palate.

Yes, there are individual differences, and some children are more naturally adventurous eaters than others. But we do our children a real disservice by taking their small nos and maybes as law.

The classic children's book *Bread and Jam for Frances* presents a young badger who never wants to try anything new. After repeatedly offering her tempting foods, her parents give up in frustration. But the end of the book finds Frances asking tearfully, "How do you know what I'll like if you won't even try me?" Maybe Rozin should add badgers to his list of animals that can teach us something about how to eat.

Who Comes to the Table

To give you an idea of the shrinkage of our home/supper life, let me recall a few cultural staples that, within my memory, have either substantially diminished or else disappeared. These institutions let us see how, in the recent past, home-cooked meals and home-based entertainments marked the center of sociability. They give a few more examples of the richness and variety that come from combining two basic needs, for nourishment and for connection. They point up opportunities missed when we plunk ourselves down, individually, with our suppers, in front of the TV.

- *Having the minister or teacher in for supper.* These traditions evolved from an earlier time, when professions were supported directly by the community. In pioneering societies, the teacher's contract would normally include room and board at a succession of local homes.
- *Inviting the boss home for supper.* This was an occasion of tremendous stress, and was seen as a test of the wife's homemaking abilities, which were thought to affect her husband's career prospects (obviously before women were expected to have careers of their own). Roast beef was considered the appropriate dish.
- *Boardinghouses.* Enterprising widows would provide workers in cities or at worksites with a room and a shared supper. The nightly meal provided a small step toward creating a family atmosphere for unrelated individuals. But the institution came with few illusions. The term *boardinghouse reach* refers to the fact that, in this collection of strangers thrown together by circumstance, if you wanted something, you'd better make a grab for it.
- *Gourmet clubs.* Small groups of couples would get together at regular intervals for elaborately

produced theme nights. Each couple would bring
one of the dishes, made from a recipe provided, or
at least in keeping with the evening's motif.
Having specific culinary expectations bumped the
couples-night-out up a notch, improving cooking
skills and offering a hint of the cosmopolitan.
· *Progressive suppers.* A group traveled from house to
house, eating one course at each home. This was
another way to inject social life with a some
variety, as well as being a way to spread the work.
· *Hosting a supper for a new arrival.* Inviting one's neighbors or social circle was a way to introduce a new-
comer and provide a social occasion for the "old
hands."

These days, invitations to eat at the houses of friends, colleagues, relatives, or neighbors are arriving less and less often.
According to Harry Balzer, vice president of The NPD Group,
which tracks food trends, in 2003 "The average American was
a guest at somebody else's house twelve times. In 1990, it was
sixteen times." That's a decline of 25 percent in just over a
decade. And when we do invite people over for supper, it's
likely to be a low-maintenance affair: ordering in pizza to watch
sports on TV, a backyard barbecue in which the actual cooking
can be handed off, most often to a male who counts this as his
only cooking skill. Much of what is eaten is finger food, and if
it's served outside, no one even has to come into the house.

As well, our households themselves have shrunk. In earlier
times, *household* meant the people who lived under the same
roof. This might have included servants, apprentices, and

assorted members of the extended family. Now households are more likely to be limited to the nuclear family, or some variation on that theme. Whenever we invite a family friend to supper, that person rises in status, becoming "almost a member of the family." Bringing in other adults enriches the experience. For children, eating at a friend's house can be an eye-opening foray into the wider world. Even the family pet understands the importance of putting in an appearance at suppertime.

John Finn, who teaches a course at Wesleyan University called Culture and Cuisine, has seen firsthand the downside of not eating together. "What's most striking is the sense of loss my students have," Finn tells me. "The vast majority don't have any real cooking skills. They have no sense of how recipes get handed down from generation to generation; of how families, and cultures, are connected by food over time; of how what we eat takes on a richness and a layering far beyond its ingredients." He says that, although TV cooking shows are popular with his students, they watch them purely as entertainment. One of his students told him how, at every major holiday, her mother would make a Boston cream pie. And now, in college, this young woman was realizing that, not only had she never learned how to make that or any other dessert, but she thought that she never would.

"The students wished their parents had involved them in the kitchen. Every year, for their term paper, probably half of a class of fifteen or twenty students wants to create a family cookbook. All this knowledge they think hasn't been handed down from their parents." Food is a direct route to the intimacies of family life.

Finn became aware of supper early. His father died when he

was a teenager, and his mother began working the evening shift as a nurse. He was responsible for making supper for his younger siblings. Now he gives his students cooking demonstrations, showing them what's possible with the microwave and plug-in grill that constitute "legal" dorm equipment. He's shown them curried turkey burger with a mint chutney sauce, and salmon fillet with balsamic maple syrup glaze. He is hoping they will prepare meals they can share with their friends.

In our contemporary world, the new addition to the dinner table might well be the mother's helper or nanny. The question of whether or not she eats with the family is a clear indication of her social status. A mother's helper of the family's own social set, or, say, a European au pair, would be expected to eat with the family (if, indeed, the family eats together at all). Whether it's her own preference or the family's choice, an au pair from the other side of a perceived social divide is more likely to eat on her own.

Some years ago, Marvin Harris wrote a fascinating book, *Good to Eat*, arguing that food taboos are not so much about food or religion as about ensuring group solidarity. If I keep kosher, or eat only Hallal foods, and you don't share my practice, it will be difficult for us to eat together. And if we can't share meals, we are less likely to be friends.

One of the most anxious-making parts of going away to college is the who-will-I-eat-with dilemma. Nervous freshmen make pacts, implicit or expressed, to eat together. It is the trauma of junior high, the test of your social worth, repeated three times a day. Nothing points up the change from home to school like the prospect of facing that huge cafeteria alone. To reprise Epicurus, "Eating alone is leading the life of a lion or wolf."

We eat with people we care about. We care about the people who share our meal. As Robert Putnam writes in *Bowling Alone*, "Since the evening meal has been a communal experience in virtually all societies for a very long time, the fact that it has visibly diminished in the course of a single generation in our country is remarkable evidence of how rapidly our social connectedness has been changing." And not for the better, if you value that kind of link. When we give up our family meal, we squander an obvious opportunity to connect.

HOW WE TALK

Supper is as much about talking as it is about eating. We have already looked at some of the things we talk about at the dinner table. But the act of talking is important in itself. To find out a bit about the mechanics of how we converse, I visit Sharon Weiss-Kapp, a speech pathologist at MGH Institute of Health Professions at Massachusetts General Hospital. Weiss-Kapp, I notice, speaks in sentences that are smooth and coherent. Her appearance, and her office, likewise seem ordered and calm. I am aware that I am choosing my words very carefully, speaking slowly and distinctly.

Weiss-Kapp explains that speech is much more than stringing together a bunch of words. It's about the subtle dance of conversation, a verbal two-step or more. It is also about logical inference, understanding context, interpreting subtext, making cognitive leaps. If supper is good for our digestions and our emotions, it also provides a workout for our minds.

She explains it this way: "If I say, It's really cold in here, you might acknowledge the literal intent: Yes, it's cold. You might say, I'm going to turn up the heat. You might say, I'm going to get you a sweater." So in real conversation, you don't always have to be explicit. You can rely on the other person's knowledge of social relations. Weiss-Kapp says cold, and I make the leap to thermostat or sweater.

She remembers one particular incident when her son was about two. When she came home, he said, "Can I have a cookie?" She responded, "Did you pick up your toys?" He asked again, "Can I have a cookie?" And she repeated, "Did you pick up your toys?"

Weiss-Kapp was thinking: *If you're finished with one activity, we can go on to the next. If you've cleaned up after yourself, then you can eat.* But her son was too young to think that abstractly, to take his mother's perspective, or see her logic.

He responded in a typically two-year-old fashion, by lying down on the floor and throwing a tantrum. She reports ruefully, "I made him crazy! He was probably thinking, *This woman has no idea what I am talking about!*"

Part of growing up is learning how to make those conversational inferences. We come to understand that the person we are talking to may share some or all of how we understand the world. If we share certain basic assumptions, then we can take shortcuts. Weiss-Kapp says, "If I talk to you about the Red Sox and you're from Boston, that's a shared association." (Great faith, years of frustration capped by recent jubilation.) But if she is talking to a British person, the Red Sox would have little meaning.

We humans have to be fleet-footed to carry on a conversation. Weiss-Kapp gives me a list of conversational rules. Their subjects include initiating conversation, turn taking, maintaining topics, changing topics, conversational repairs, and requesting clarification. We have to learn how to start talking, how to keep talking, when to talk about something else, when to stop talking altogether. We also have to learn the particular rules that govern our cultural subgroup and our family.

Some families wait for one person to finish speaking before another begins. In other clans, everyone chimes in at once. Weiss-Kapp tells me that, in her family of origin, people were encouraged to interrupt, a style she calls cross-talking. They then felt like the conversation was lively, with everyone engaged. This sort of overlapping conversation can also be about power and control. (If I interrupt you but you don't interrupt me, then eventually I will monopolize the conversation — a sign that I'm in a position of power over you.) Weiss-Kapp still remembers her shock when her kindergarten teacher reported to her parents that she always interrupted.

In addition to learning the conversational do-si-do, the structure of conversation, we also learn how to tell stories. As we've seen, stories are family glue, correlating with resilience. *How* we tell them matters as well. Now, these can be very small tales — *I tried a new recipe; Guess who I ran into today* — but they must follow rules of narrative, with a protagonist, a beginning, a middle, and an end. One of the reasons it can be so mind numbing to listen to a child's recitation of, say, the plot of a movie she's just seen, is that kids have not yet learned to pick out the salient features. They haven't learned to synthesize or condense, but insist on telling every last teeny detail.

At the supper table, kids learn to tell stories by listening. The adults also engage them in direct conversation, giving them a chance to practice their skills.

"You ask your husband, What happened when you got to work, what did you do at lunch, when did your day end," Weiss-Kapp explains. "A child says, I get it, there's a beginning, a middle, and an end."

Which can be why the question *What did you do today?* may be met with shrugs and grunts. *What did you do today* is just too big a topic. Children don't know what's important — which part they should pick out, where they should start, what part of the *do* or *today* can give them the entry point to the narrative. It helps if you "scaffold" — give children some structure, break apart your question. *Who did you see today? In math, did you do addition or multiplication?* Instead of giving them a blank slate, give them a choice. And then, Weiss-Kapp says, "Repeat back to them — Oh, you did your multiplication? Did you have trouble? Did you feel frustrated? Maybe you could get help from your teacher." She calls this modeling, so that kids learn not just to speak, but to converse. She also calls it an enriched environment. "Lots of language and lots of experience — that's the best thing you can do for a child."

Weiss-Kapp says that supper "sort of forces an environment when everyone has to stop and sit down. It creates a boundary when you're sitting around a table. It's a designated time. It focuses attention on what is going on here and now between the people around the table. It gives us a specific time to review our day." The event, like narrative itself, has a beginning, a middle, and an end, so children can anticipate how long it's going to take.

She makes the point that, when children are acquiring any kind of skill, the most important thing they can do is practice, practice, practice. Also, when learning a new skill, there's a huge level of comfort in predictability. Because supper happens every day, it makes an excellent learning ground. Kids can try out their skills, improving them from night to night.

Which is one reason why we should turn off that TV. If you're watching, then you're not talking. You're not engaging the child in conversation. You're passing up a great opportunity.

Take that one step farther: What happens if you're not even home for supper, but rather driving your kid to his next commitment and feeding him chicken nuggets in the car?

"There's a sense of pressure," Weiss-Kapp says. "It's very frantic. If you're driving, your attention is divided. Talk about maintaining topic! It's going to be about requests and protests, not about commenting." And, she elaborates, "Commenting is what's going on to move the conversation forward." No conversation is going to go forward between the red lights and the spilled fries.

Weiss-Kapp explains this all to me in a very clear and orderly way. I can see why she enjoys this work; she has a strong sense of structure. When we begin to wrap up the interview, she says, "For closing, I'll show you pictures of my kids." The snapshot she keeps on her windowsill shows her daughter standing at the dinner table.

Coincidence? She laughs, and says, "We're always there."

Weiss-Kapp tells me that she and her husband always have supper together (the kids are now in college, so it's just the two of them). When the kids were at home, they always ate family supper. Her children didn't do a lot of sports or extracurricular activities, so scheduling wasn't a problem.

Didn't do a lot of extracurriculars? In her high-end suburb, this must have raised a red flag. When I ask if she worried about that, she doesn't apologize, doesn't elaborate, doesn't even blink. "No," she says, and smiles. I happen to know, from a common friend, that her kids are doing well; that her home, like her office, is calm and well ordered. Weiss-Kapp confirms that her husband arrives home on the same train every night.

I get a sense of their family dinners unfolding in their smooth way, in their own good time, with lots of relaxed but engaging cross-talk. It occurs to me that Weiss-Kapp's calm consistency, her family's access to each other every night, her confidence that her kids would do fine even if they didn't knock themselves out signing up for extracurriculars, might have done them as much good as being on any number of teams.

FIVE O'CLOCK SHADOW

If you look at supper from a time-management point of view, it's a setup for disaster. We straggle homeward, blood sugar down, blood pressure spiking. Social scientists call it "domestic reentry," as if, after floating through space with clusters of twinkling stars, we have to subject ourselves to earth's leaden orbit again. Adults who have spent the day zooming around on overdrive have to pull back to present at least an appearance of calm. Teenagers need to shift from the high-energy rhythms and gnawing insecurities of teendom to the more staid behavioral expectations of parents. Youngsters are finally free to crash after a day of being expected to behave, behave, behave.

Safe at home, we let whatever unseemly behavior we have managed to keep in check all day come oozing out. Anyone who has dragged an exhausted child screaming from day care, a child who insists that he wants to stay with his friends, that he doesn't want to go home with you, knows why this is called the witching hour. We shed our masks along with our jackets, briefcases, and backpacks.

This is the time when we all want to be mothered. But Mom cannot relax. She has to gear up for the big push to get supper on the table asap, with a minimum of time, energy, and intrafamilial bloodletting. (One mother calls it "cooking with whine.") Despite a generation of advancement for women in terms of jobs, politics, and personal choices, when the clock hands point to supper, it can look like women haven't made many gains at all. Even though Mom no longer wears the flowered apron, she is still facing a particularly intractable second-wave feminist conundrum. The folks who study things like time allocation and shifting roles call it "doing gender."

Because contemporary apron strings include the cell phone, the computer, and the centrally located family calendar, Mom is never "off." And suppertime is when many different needs converge. Women still "own" mealtime, even if the food handling has become more sanitized, less physical. No matter that they work, either part time or full, women have continued to be primarily responsible for the home, shouldering the burden of the second shift.

This inequality forms the backdrop of a 1994 study by Reed Larson, a psychologist at the University of Illinois. To find out how time and emotions play out within the family over the course of the day, he studied fifty-five two-parent working- and middle-class families in suburban Chicago, all of whom had, at the least, a child in fifth through eighth grade. Study participants kept time diaries for a week. They also carried pagers so researchers could beep them to find out what they were doing and how they were feeling at any given time.

It's not surprising that mothers with full-time jobs reported spending more total time on labor than did mothers who worked part time or mothers who were not employed. Working mothers also clocked more hours than did working husbands. What's unsettling is that, Larson says, "Men's input to family labor varied little as a function of their wives' employment, suggesting that they did not increase their household contribution to reduce the double-shift of job and family work carried by their wives." Roughly speaking, men did the same amount of household work regardless of the employment status of their wives.

So how did the Chicago families feel about it all? When the psychologists beeped the parents during the end-of-the-workday, right-before-supper witching hour, the wife could most often be found working in the kitchen, while her husband was most often relaxing in front of the TV. And it gets even worse. "We found that husbands' negative emotional states at the end of the day at work often predicted their wives' emotions on the first report at home — in the middle of this high-demand period." In other words, the guys who came home stressed out by work transmitted their bad feelings to their wives. But the opposite did not happen. Men were unaffected by their wives' emotional states.

The employed women "had greater average daily happiness than other women." But how did their happiness play out over the course of the day? They were "comparatively happy when they were at work. But when they came home to their families in the evening their average emotional state fell substantially. . . . These mothers tended to experience what we have called the 'Six O'Clock Crash.' (In contrast, their husbands' emotions rose during this period.)"

Uh-oh; let's make sure we're getting this right. Women's spirits drooped when they came home and had to deal with the needs of their families, first of which was an evening meal, at a time when their husbands were taking a break and feeling good. So for a woman, supper becomes the clash of two cultures: the time when her modern working-woman identity butts heads with her old nurturing role.

Interestingly enough, a way out of this conundrum may come from people who are even more burdened — single mothers.

In 1999, Larson studied 101 middle-class single mothers of adolescents. "The employed single mothers did not differ significantly from employed two-parent mothers in their average amount of time at their jobs, but they reported less time in family work (a mean of 15.6 percent of their time, as compared to 21.3 percent for the two-parent mothers)." Less time in family work? Shouldn't the single mothers be doing more?

They did do slightly more housework, Larson says, but, "time on child care activities did not differ significantly between the two groups. . . . Other studies have had similar findings: that one-parent mothers generally do less total family work than similar two-parent mothers."

One explanation might be that, for housework, simply removing the husband/partner/father figure means less cooking, shopping, cleaning, and so on, because there is one less adult. (And we have already established that, in household terms, on average, a man is a make-work proposition.)

Larson doesn't go down that path. He says he first thought that the difference occurred because, in single-parent families, children take on more work, but his studies found that this wasn't the case. The kids were not taking up the slack.

He came up with a different and intriguing explanation: The absence of a husband reduces expectations. "When there is no man in the home, I suspect, there may be lower expectations for immaculate cleanliness, elaborate meals, and other nonessential products of mothers' labor, at least in many households." So the single mothers can set their own standards, at their own pace.

A chart that compares Mean Happiness Across Hours of the Weekday between single mothers and married mothers shows two very different patterns. Where married mothers' happiness peaks at about 1:30 P.M., and then shoots down to reach its nadir between 5:30 and 7:30, single mothers report a much more even line that dips slightly between 3:30 and 5:30 before rising steeply. They actually feel better when they come home. Married mothers report being happier during the day, but single mothers report greater happiness in the evening. Larson's explanation is that, because single moms have lower expectations, they can be more flexible, changing household routines to suit their particular circumstances. This idea is borne out by his second chart, which shows when families eat dinner in the two types of households. In the two-parent households, the "shared meal" line spikes dramatically. Fifty-nine percent eat between 5:30 and 6:30 P.M. In the one-parent families, however, the evening meal was likely to occur anytime between 4:30 and 8:30.

The lesson we can learn from all this? Tell the guys to tone down the expectations and pump up the active engagement. Let's retire that supermom idea once and for all. Maybe we should get creative about that end-of-the-day pileup. Maybe we need to step back, see who actually needs what at that time, and rejigger our schedules. Maybe Mom needs a bit of quiet time. Maybe we should all be more responsible, not leave the heavy lifting up to the female parent. Maybe we should eat early. Maybe we should snack early and then eat late. Maybe the older kids should cook. Maybe the dad should. Maybe we should think hard and long about modern motherhood.

That's what Teresa Arendell, a Colby College–based sociologist, has been doing. She studied middle-class mothers in northern California to find out how they made it all work — the doctors' appointments, the carpools, the suppers, the day camps, the internships, the jobs. She notes that, in preparation for their meeting, one woman told her, "You'll know who I am; I'm the one who looks frazzled." But that woman was wrong, Arendell says. All the mothers she interviewed had that grim look.

In our postindustrial educational society, children's time is highly structured. There is a focus on individualization, and a major investment, by the parents, of time, energy, and money to keep their children on the go. Arendell contends that the energy and time are expended primarily by the mother. Time is the currency of our service and knowledge society — a commodity so rare that it has changed how we think about work, leisure, and wealth. We no longer have enough time to squander it or waste it; even children must invest their time in something with payoff potential. For modern parents, time equals caring. And women shoulder much more of this burden of time.

In *The 1997 National Study of the Changing Workforce*, researchers found that "Married mothers report spending nearly an hour more than fathers each workday 'caring for and doing things with' their children (3.2 vs. 2.3 hours). On days off, the difference grows to nearly two hours per day, with mothers spending 8.3 hours and fathers 6.4 hours." In this study, it must be said, fathers average about 10.5 hours more time at work per week, which we must assume contributes to the family coffers.

But here's the strange thing: Even though most women are working, the expectations of motherhood are shooting higher; the job description is becoming more demanding and complex. First, there are the hearth-and-home demands. Our houses are twice as big as they were fifty years ago. Somebody has to take care of them, arrange for maintenance, cleaning, decoration, and repairs. That tends to be woman's work. And to fill those big houses, we own more stuff that has to be bought, maintained, thrown out, replaced. Most often, that's woman's work, too.

And then there are the children. As Arendell says, "A child has not only particular physical, emotional, and moral claims on the mother, but also educational and enrichment ones. Such parenting is deeply labor intensive and necessitates a high degree of intimate knowledge about each child, his or her interests, abilities, temperament, and developmental 'progress.'" And the children's time must be crammed full; again, mother's job. According to researchers at the University of Michigan, in 1981 the average child could count 40 percent of his day's activities as discretionary. By 1997, that had dropped to 25 percent. In that same period, the amount of time spent on eating declined about 20 percent on weekdays. Did children learn to eat faster? Or did we just spend less time sitting around together at the table?

Arendell explains that intensive parenting is now the norm. "*Good* childhoods are intended not only to secure children's immediate psychological well-being and growth. They also aim to prepare children for their future roles as adults. . . . Steady involvement in organized enrichment activities enhances and secures children's individual *cultural capital*, readying them for participation in select strata of adult life." Or, as we all know, a child who doesn't play soccer, study oboe, and work at the soup kitchen, preferably all on the same day, can just kiss Harvard good-bye.

Add to this mothers' absence from home during the day, and the pervasive, if not necessarily realistic, fears about children's safety, and you have the explosion of extracurricular activities that define contemporary childhood. And who researches the programs; keeps track of each child's abilities, needs, and predilections; organizes the carpools; and then worries about it all? The moms. If they are no longer cooking or sewing or knitting or shopping or cleaning house, then by God they are managing. They are the keepers of the calendars. As one of Arendell's subjects said, "I'm the queen of colored pens."

Not that this is forced labor. By managing their families' time, Arendell says, mothers have been able to exert a decent amount of control over their families' lives. But it has come at the expense of couple time and personal time. And society at large is not helping. "Workplace structure and dynamics go largely unchallenged, and women are left to manage on their own. . . .

"Mothers often are blamed in the popular culture for the speed-up in children's lives, for an overemphasis on structured activities over self-initiated play and other pursuits, and for, supposedly, engaging in a competition with other families over children's attainments and successes." But,

Arendell says, what we fail to appreciate is that what mothers do serves the larger public interest. "Children are socialized into and prepared for the adult world where the demands of productivity, success, competitiveness, and flexibility are universal. Also universal is the escalation of time."

As a society, and as families, we want our children to be productive and efficient — good managers, team players, talented, well-rounded individualists. But much of this has come at the expense of family life. And it all comes crashing down at the end of the day. Just when we need the predictability, the warmth, the quiet acceptance that comes from some unpressured together time, what do we get? The steam rising in the pressure cooker that is the American family today.

My sociologist friend Jeanne tells me that the term *cultural capital* has a very specific provenance. It's about parents investing in their children so the children can be worth more. But are we so obsessed with our narrow, anxious view of our children's future that we throw away the riches we can offer them now? How about the pleasure that they give to us? If home runs on factory time, if we are forever measuring our output, then we might as well just stay at work. At least there, women can expect an equitable distribution of tasks.

Supper can be the anti-stress, anti-management, anti-need-to-excel pill. It can provide the fix of warmth/nurturing/relaxation/enjoyment we so badly need. Let's just not leave it all up to Mom.

Full disclosure: As someone who pleads guilty to keeping control of the evening meal in her tight little hands, I know that moms also have to learn to let go. And so I suggest: Make a chart. Ask for help. Stop thinking of it as help. Reapportion the end-of-day tasks so that there is real sharing of the work-load. Let's learn from the single moms. Reduce expectations. Share the chores.

When We Eat

Children tend to come home from school either hungry or else very hungry. They may not have eaten much lunch, the school cafeteria having been too noisy, too chaotic, too social, too full of the wrong smells. But if kids fill up on snacks when they get home, they will not be very hungry at supper. However, they *will* be hungry again when it is time to go to bed.

If we want to avoid this scenario, we must pay attention to our children's, and our, eating schedule in its entirety. For kids who arrive home ravenous, think of easy-access, nourishing snacks — a bowl of soup, a sandwich, or something like yogurt, a banana, and nuts. Just try to make sure they don't eat so much that they lose interest in supper.

Families who want to eat their evening meal together, but have members who don't come home until late, have to make a difficult choice. Should everyone wait for the late arrival? Should the kids eat first, maybe saving dessert (or tea, or milk) until the latecomer gets home? Some older kids and teenagers do fine with a late meal if they've been fortified by a healthy snack. For younger kids, however, you are probably looking for trouble. Evening time is homework time, and nobody works well with a low blood sugar level and a growling stomach, not to mention that by the time you do get to the table together, the kids will probably be cranky and ready for bed. It's a lousy trade-off.

One approach is to try to increase the intake of healthy foods throughout the day, so that the evening's caloric demands do not loom so large. Make leftovers available for breakfast. Talk with your kids on an ongoing basis about what they are eating for lunch. Get creative about those after-school snacks. Foods you put together yourself have more of a potential for some reasonable nutritional value. Outside the home, snacks are the impulse buys of the food world. We spend too much on them in terms of calories, and get the least benefit from them in terms of nutrition.

One of the benefits of eating meals together is that it's a natural time to talk about food. When kids hear adults discussing what they are eating now, what they have eaten over the course of the day, they will (hopefully) learn how to make good choices. As well, by agreeing to eat together at a particular time, we limit our eating in the hours before and after the meal. I have mentioned before that one of the benefits/ requirements of eating together is showing up hungry. Supper is only one time in our day, but it affects how we structure our other time.

WHERE WE EAT . . . AND WHERE NOT TO

The question of what it means to eat in different places — kitchen, dining room, bedroom, restaurant, car — continues to puzzle me. So I call Witold Rybczynski, an original thinker who has written several fascinating books about the meaning of home and a sense of place. Surely, I think, if anyone can help me understand this question, Rybczynski is the one. But his response is so simple, and so obvious, that I am brought up short. "We eat facing each other," he says. Period. I ask my question again, in a different way. "It's the facing each other that's important," he repeats.

As he turns the topic over, examining it from a variety of angles, he does not change his mind. The distinctions between different rooms, or whether we eat at home or in a commercial establishment, are not critical, he insists. It's the fact of sitting face-to-face, inviting interaction, give-and-take, that matters most.

So if we want a significant social experience, or at least the possibility of one, it is our body posture vis-à-vis our companions that is all-important. We can be squatting on a jungle floor, perched cross-legged on carpets in a desert tent, ringing a campfire in the middle of the woods, or sitting around a Formica table in a fast-food eatery.

By contrast, the diners at medieval banquets sat in a row along one side of a very long table. Their purpose, in addition to getting something to eat, was not to converse with their tablemates, but to illustrate their status. The more important people sat at one end of the table, the less important down at the other end. The salt was placed in the center. The expression *below the salt* persists centuries after this form of social display has fallen into disuse.

But at least those placed below the salt were sitting at the table. Because, while they ate, using their hands, knives, or flat pieces of stale bread called trenchers to scoop up their food, their social inferiors were standing across from them, back beyond the empty edge of the table. The peasants stood and watched their "betters" eat. This was pretty straightforward consumption-as-status. After the meal, the members of the lower orders got the leftovers.

But let's not be too quick to dismiss our status-conscious ancestors. Don't the seats around our own, more modest family tables have status markers of their own? Woe to the visitor who unwittingly sits in what my friend Jeanne, the sociologist, calls the alpha male's chair. What about all those sibling fights over who gets the "good" seat?

From our more immediate past, we conjure up an image of a farmhouse kitchen, its center a big table that always has room for one more. But in the contemporary version of the "farmhouse kitchen," that central table sometimes disappears. We install a double sink, side-by-side refrigerator-freezer, a special fridge just for wine. These rooms are set up for staff: either the nanny/cook/housekeeper of upscale households, or the caterer hired for special occasions by the homeowners of the next level down. For family eating, you will often find a counter. The kids pull up stools for their on-demand snacks and instant meals.

In commercial eateries in our era, sitting in a line means watching a show, not being part of one. New York luncheon-ettes have retained their counters, where solitary diners can enjoy the smooth, efficient movements of the grill tenders and sandwich makers. Sushi bars have the same appeal. Some sushi joints add an extra treat — individual dishes that move on slow, continuous tracks. Diners grab the plate they want, then stack up the color-coded empties in front of them, to be tabulated when it's time for the bill.

When my husband and I stop for supper to break up a long car ride, we have discovered the allure of eating at the bar. After hours alone together in the car, we have nothing left to say to each other, so it's great to have the stimulation and distraction of watching the bartender, the other customers, the silent TV.

But that's not the effect you want to conjure at your standard family evening meal. This is, for many families, the only time in the day when everyone is at the same place at the same time doing the same thing. Rybczynski says, "You do need to stop and sit down and form this group for the meal to have all these functions. It has a kind of primeval aspect to it. The table, even a circle of people sitting on the floor, gives a temporary sense of privacy." Even if there's nobody else around, our formation, facing each other, helps us to cohere.

He tells me that, if he's grabbing a sandwich in the kitchen at lunchtime, his wife gets upset if he eats it standing up. There's something profoundly unsociable about this posture. He considers for a minute, then says, "I think she's right."

He and his wife have also agreed on the amount of distraction they will accept at their meals. No TV or reading at the table, except for two instances: "We watch *60 Minutes*. We read the Sunday paper at lunchtime. We're both very conscious this is some kind of exception . . . the only time we're allowed to do it."

He doesn't make a distinction between watching TV and reading at the table. He gives the example of the standard movie scene that shows a couple at breakfast hiding behind their newspapers. "It's never saying a good thing," he says. "It's always a mark of something about to go wrong."

So Rybczynski isn't exercised about whether people eat in the kitchen, the family room, or the dining room, as long as they are face-to-face. He sees the dining room, or lack thereof, as a class issue, and formality or informality as not meaning much. "It's like dressing for dinner," he says. "If you were upper class it was automatic. Then, at some point, it stopped. Social habit."

In cramped city apartments, the dining room has long been the first casualty of the space wars, the most obvious spot to be turned into an extra bedroom or office. In contemporary houses, the dining room is not necessarily part of the plan at all; its space has been subsumed into the "great room" — one all-purpose cooking/eating/gathering space.

But here is the thing: When our eating table is used for many different purposes, we need to rededicate it to its primary function when mealtime rolls around. When we are ready to eat, we should have a table free of homework, bills, science projects, not to mention assorted stacks of who-knows-what stuff. This clearing-the-decks helps to create that frame around the meal, that time-out-of-time. Thus we eat at a place dedicated to eating, even though, half an hour before, it might have been an office. That is why, even though they are old-fashioned, too-formal space wasters, dining rooms have not disappeared entirely. They remind us of the importance of getting together for a meal.

Also: Nutritionists tell us that we shouldn't eat all over the house. You want to become your own inner Pavlov. Train yourself to understand that the kitchen or dining room means eating, and that other locations just don't. One of the big culprits in our epidemic of expanding waistlines is the total, constant availability of food. One obvious way to limit our opportunities to consume is to restrict where we eat. No snacking on the street; no walking around mindlessly munching. No stuffing our faces in front of the TV. Eat at mealtimes. Eat in society.

Here is what Marjorie Garber has to say in her book with the brilliant title of *Sex and Real Estate*: "Perhaps increasingly, for busy people, space has come to substitute for time, and the house becomes the unlived life. In an era when the 'welcome mat' and the 'answering machine' all-too-often stand in for personal greeting and the human voice, the house — with its 'living' room, 'dining' room, 'family' room and 'media' room, is the place where we stage the life we wish we had time to live."

Contemporary Americans have oodles of space. But we are starved for time, particularly the time, and the occasion, to connect. So let's keep Rybczynski's simple, yet complex advice in mind. *Where* we eat is not critically important. What makes the difference is that we use the opportunity to join together in a life-sustaining and pleasurable endeavor (eating), which echoes with endless shared associations. To get the most out of any meal, eat facing each other.

As to Where Not to Eat — please, please, not in the car. And not in front of the TV. I can understand the appeal of sitting in the backseat of a vehicle moving through the dark, plunging ketchupy fingers into a bag full of fries and then licking off the fat, salty warmth. It's anonymous. It's denlike. It's infantile.

Which is the problem. You turn from an eater into a feeder, stuffing food into your mouth without awareness of how much you're eating. You separate the act of eating from the act of preparation. (The food appears at the drive-in window; the remains get stuffed into the trash.) Also, the food is likely to fall onto your lap and stain your clothes. The drinks will spill onto the seats and seep into the carpets; the crumbs will slip into folds and cracks that the coin-operated vacuum wand can never reach. Your car will forever smell like a take-out window.

Generations of children have been warned to never, never let a stranger lure them into a car with the promise of a treat. But parents use this tactic all the time with their dear ones. I am told that food-in-the-car is the standard ploy used to pry a child out of day care for the trip home. The bottle, the sippy-cup, the apple, the doughnut, the Happy Meal — all do their part to establish the neural connection, *Car equals food; car riding equals eating.*

You are doing your child no favors. Although it's hard to picture now, one day your little darling will be a middle-age person with a slowing metabolism and a spreading waistline, while her brain continues to whisper *car, eating; car, food. If I am in my vehicle,* she will be thinking, *it must be time for a little something.*

As for the whole family eating entire meals in the car, please consider that it will take you only an extra quarter of an hour to consume that same meal inside the restaurant. You will sit facing each other. You might even say something to each other, listen to each other, enjoy a bit of each other's company. Can you really not afford fifteen minutes for the good, and the pleasure, of your family, not to mention stretching your legs? How about getting take-out, but finding a park with a picnic table, or spreading your meal out on the grass? Look around you. Take a deep breath. Don't you feel better already?

Can I even suggest that you take the food home? Build up those connections: *Home = nurturing. Home = satisfaction. Home = a full-stomached feeling of contentment.* Consider the Hebrew proverb, *Spread the table and the quarrel will end.* Or the South African one: *When you have a lot to do, start with a meal.*

When you do eat at home, if you are thinking about pulling up your tray to eat your supper in front of the tube, I hope that the links among TV, calories, and dollars will make you think twice.

In 1988, researchers at the Children's Nutrition Research Center (CNRC) at Baylor University in Houston ran a study to see whether watching TV during meals was related to obesity. They asked 287 fourth-, fifth-, and sixth-graders in the Houston area to keep track of the food they ate over the course of a week. This sample was nicely varied by ethnicity. The researchers also knew these students' Body Mass Index (BMI), and so could measure their relative level of obesity. Of the 1,775 dinners recorded, 42 percent were eaten in front of the TV.

They found that kids who were overweight ate 50 percent of their dinners in front of the tube while, for normal-weight children, the number was 35 percent. Do I have your attention now?

According to Karen Cullen, a CNRC behavioral nutritionist and Baylor assistant professor of pediatrics, "We know there's a link between the number of hours children watch television and weight problems. We also know that people who watch television while eating tend to tune out their natural hunger and satiety cues, which encourages overeating." We sit there like zombies, moving our hands automatically from the bag of chips to our mouths, while our attention is elsewhere. This is a very different way to eat than putting a set amount of food on a plate, putting that plate on a table, and then sitting around the table with other people.

In addition to influencing how we eat, TV plays a big part in *what* we eat. Cullen says, "The foods most heavily advertised tend to be low in nutritional value." There is much less incentive to advertise unprocessed foods such as fruits, vegetables, or plain sources of protein, which have less markup. The biggest profits come from the most highly processed foods — those items with the most additives, and the most marketing tie-ins.

As Kelly D. Brownell reported in his 2004 book *Food Fight*, "At its peak, the 5 A Day fruit and vegetable program from the National Cancer Institute had $2 million for promotion. This is one-fifth the $10 million used annually to advertise Altoids mints. In turn, the Altoids budget is a speck compared to budgets for the big players — $3 billion in 2001 for Coca-Cola and PepsiCo combined just for the United States." When you think about product tie-ins, and children's relative innocence in assessing food claims, you can see how they make a very tempting target for the producers of highly processed, highly sugared, nutritionally questionable foods.

A fascinating perspective on dollars, cents, nutrition, and health comes from a 2003 working paper by three economists from the Institute of Economic Research at Harvard, *Why Have Americans Become More Obese*. It addresses the question of how the United States became the fattest nation in the world, and why supper can be part of the way out of our current fix.

The paper's authors, David Cutler, Edward Glaesner, and Jesse Shapiro, decided to use their skills at logical thinking and number crunching to get a bead on the obesity epidemic. Their premise is that, because people are notoriously inaccurate about reporting their eating habits to researchers, those standard what-do-you-eat methods can't be trusted. Even the fact of keeping a food diary for a few days will have an effect on what people consume. So they extrapolated backward from the amount of food produced and consumed in the past generation, and correlated it with weight tables to see how much, and what, foods were being eaten.

They use the potato as an example. Although, before World War II, Americans ate "massive" amounts of potatoes, these were usually baked, boiled, or mashed, and were generally cooked at home. Between 1977 and 1995, consumption of potatoes increased 30 percent, but almost entirely in the form of french fries and potato chips, those twin demons of reasonable nutrition.

They also bring up cream cakes. Filled cakes have long been common, but making them is time consuming and even forces the home baker to expend a few calories in their production. These days, they are mass produced, cheap, and widely available: the type of highly processed, widely advertised food that we grab when we're looking for a pick-me-up or a treat.

These foods are bad for us, but they are profitable. "Eighty per cent of the cost of food eaten at home is now spent on non–farm related expenses," the paper says. "Labor in the supermarket and the factory has replaced labor in the home."

As for our national weight gain, the Harvard economists argue that we haven't dramatically changed the amount that we eat at meals. We have, rather, increased the amount we eat between meals. Food is now available everywhere, all the time — in vending machines, in kiosks, in stores of all types, in cultural institutions. And the foods we eat as snacks are the most highly processed, heavily advertised, and calorie dense — the ones most advertised on TV.

Which is another argument for supper. As I have said, an important part of eating meals together is showing up hungry. If you know you are expected for dinner, then, both before and after the meal, you will eat fewer snacks. And if snacks are the most densely caloric, least nutritious parts of our diet, then supper looks very good. When eating is a social activity, we are limited to eating in only certain situations. If we are free to eat anything, anytime, anywhere, with no one keeping an eye out for the amount or quality of what we consume, it is easy to see how our weight will balloon.

It is also an argument for having the family all eat the same meal. When cooking for a group, it makes more sense to do more of the food preparation in-house. Cooking for a crowd is cheaper if you do it yourself. If, on the other hand, each family member is eating something different, it's more tempting to go for the individual heat-and-serve dishes.

So, where to eat? Facing each other. Not in the car. Not in front of the TV. *Bon appétit!*

Manners: Building Character . . . and Civilization

It is easy to denigrate manners. They are phony, petty, prissy, and insincere. Even worse, when we teach them to our children, we can hear ourselves turning into the kind of people we'd rather not be. Who wants to be out on endless behavior patrol, burdening our children's dear, free spirits? Surely not us.

Mealtimes are where it all comes out. Seated around the table, up close to each other, our smallest actions play out in bold relief — human relationships in miniature. It is sooo obvious that, if you love almonds, and proceed to pick all of them out of the stir-fry with your fingers, there will be none left for anyone else. If you cannot stand almonds and spit a half-chewed nut on your plate, it will gross out your companions. Should you wipe your nose with your hand, your tablemates will see you and be disgusted. Conversely, if you offer the serving dish to your neighbor first, you are expressing confidence that he will leave enough for you; that the two of you are living in peacetime, in an economy of abundance.

Manners are a mini social contract, a hedge against confusion and anarchy, the manifestations of the journey from the infant tyrant to the good citizen who can give as well as receive. The French call the "before" version *le petit moi je* (the little me, I). That's the kind of person who says, Me; I want this, and I want it now. And while we accept that type of autocratic behavior from babies, a fair part of what children learn is more evenhanded ways of interacting. Which is what manners are: long-established, generally accepted phrases and actions we can fall back on so we don't have to think through every interaction every time. Should we say, Please pass the potatoes, or just do the boardinghouse reach? The long grab is fine in lots of families, at lots of social situations. At a formal dinner, it would be a disgrace.

Manners are shorthand ways of being sensitive to our surroundings. They teach consequences, highlight relationships, confirm the person's place in community. They both mold and express character.

Children learn manners mostly by example. It's only when they don't pick up on some detail that we must point out their lapses, either cheerfully and calmly, or else, in more recalcitrant cases, by nagging. (See above, the kind of person you don't want to become.) But we don't have to feel too guilty, because manners are a cut-to-the-chase way of teaching important life lessons.

When you say, Don't grab, let your brother go first, you are teaching reciprocity and empathy. When you tell your kid to sit up and quit squirming, to keep his hands to himself, you are letting him know that dinner is a particular time set aside for a particular function (eating accompanied by sociability). We have certain expectations, and we have the confidence that our children can meet them (age appropriate, of course). By teaching the actions and the words, we put our children into the social script, with the right sounds coming out of their mouths. Understanding may or may not follow. But they will have learned how to wend their way through a graceful reciprocal dance: You do this, and I will do that.

You can take it a step farther: Manners work precisely because understanding is *not* required. They represent a fallback position, a default. (*Should I pour some water into my glass, or should I just drink from the pitcher? Hmmmm.*) If your parents have drilled and nagged and reminded ad nauseum, then eventually you just do what "comes naturally." And what comes naturally will be right, at least in your social circle. You will treat your neighbor with kindness. You will make the other person feel welcome. You will not disgust the fellow sitting across the table from you. You will fit into your community. People will want to have you around.

Which is all very nicey nicey, but we should also understand that manners, especially table manners, have a much darker side. They descend directly from some of our most ancient human institutions. And they are about the Big Issues — prohibiting violence, ensuring family and group survival, drawing the line between us and them. It is no accident that we talk about "civilizing" our children. Because it is manners that helped to civilize us.

Long ago, when those hairy, small-brained, long-limbed hominid hunters made their hungry way across the tundra stalking huge scary animals, they used all their wit, determination, and primitive tools to make a kill. And when they got lucky, what did they do? Did they gorge themselves on the meat of the great woolly creature and let the rest rot? No; they cut it up and carried it back home, where they shared it out with the others who were waiting in camp. From our earliest days as a species, we have repeatedly shared our food, whether hunted, gathered, farmed, or bought at the store.

The fact that humans, of all creatures, learned to control fire added to the appeal of eating communally. It's just as much work to build a fire for a family as for an individual. And because cooking foods destroys many toxins, the combination of fire and food contributed to human health as well as sociability.

You can easily imagine the myriad variations, the way these sharing impulses have been codified down through the centuries and around the world. Many societies specify which cuts of meat go to whom; they carefully apportion the strips of blubber or ears of corn: how much to the gods, how much to the next-door neighbors, how much to the first cousins, how much to my uncle's wife's sister's kids.

The sociologist Margaret Visser says that those early shared feasts "helped give rise to many basic human characteristics, such as kinship systems (who belongs with whom; which people eat together), language (for discussing food past, present, and future, for planning the acquisition of food, and deciding how to divide it out while preventing fights), technology (how to kill, cut, keep, and carry), and morality (what is a just slice?)."

You can watch this systematized sharing play out around our own tables today. Even in informal families, the guest gets served first, or is offered the choicest morsel. After the guest, in some households the elder receives the tender bit; in other homes the children demand their favorite part. Chinese children are expected to feed their parents. A generation or two ago in the United States, everyone "knew" that children were to be seen and not heard. Now everyone "knows" that children need constant reinforcement if they are to develop that all-important self-esteem.

Manners show us the power structure, putting our values on display. Is there a little autocrat at our table? Do we live in a democracy? An oligarchy? An anarchic free-for-all? Is one family member the designated doormat, hero, or victim? Do we all defer to the sick one, the strong one, the bully, the most respected, the best loved? The best anecdote I heard about family hierarchies was about a mother who asked one of her children to switch seats with her sibling because, although both youngsters were perfectly healthy, the sibling was sitting in a draft.

Visser points out another way our human history is still present at our tables, and it is not a pretty thought. A recurrent theme of what has come down to us as prissy etiquette derives from a need to prevent violence among diners. Notice how knives are turned in toward the plate, never out toward our companion. Or the way we are not supposed to gesture toward a tablemate while holding a (potentially dangerous) knife or fork. How about the way we are told to keep our mouths closed while we chew, never showing our teeth? In the same vein, the story goes that the reason Chinese teacups don't have handles is that, with both hands on the cup, the tea drinker cannot hold a threatening knife. Evidently the potential for injury, even cannibalism, remains in the back of our collective mind.

In the 1930s, at a time when the forces of civilization were arraying themselves against a systematized brutality, Norbert Elias, a penniless German-Jewish refugee, sat in the Reading Room of the British Museum in London for three years, writing a book called *The Civilizing Process*. In it, he showed how a change in manners had gone hand in hand with the historical change from monarchy to nation-state, a more "civilized" form of government. He contended that the way people acted in daily life echoed the way they acted in the public sphere, and vice versa.

According to Elias, during the Middle Ages people at all levels of society acted more impulsively than we do now; they also had a much less developed sense of privacy. They relieved themselves in public; at table they shared dishes, goblets, knives, and spoons (forks were not used, even by the upper classes, until the seventeenth century).

Elias argued that one of the great changes of the Renaissance was the establishment of a sense of privacy that was linked to a sense of shame. People at all levels of society began to control their bodily functions in public. Spitting, nose blowing, belching, farting, and defecating became private acts. Instead of sharing table implements, people began to each use their own. They learned to sit in ways that made it unlikely they would touch each other. Elias linked these increasing controls of physicality to the controls established by the new nation-states. Governmental control passed from feuding local warlords to centralized monarchies.

With time, these behavior controls were internalized and accepted as "natural," after which they no longer had to be taught to adults, but only to successive generations of children. The examples that Elias chose from medieval advice books are the types of things that, in our world, adults take for granted:

> A man of refinement should not slurp from the same spoon with somebody else. . . .
> A man who clears his throat when he eats and one who blows his nose in the tablecloth are both ill-bred, I assure you. . . .
> A number of people gnaw a bone and then put it back in the dish — this is a serious offense.
> Those who like mustard and salt should take care to avoid the filthy habit of putting their fingers into them.

Elias argued that this change in expected behavior, this need to "civilize" each new generation, set the stage for the invention of childhood. For the first time, children were seen as being separate, not just miniature adults.

Once childhood was split off, Enlightenment intellectuals became fascinated with it, considering it a "pure" state. They wondered what language children might speak naturally; would it be Greek? The eighteenth century witnessed an obsession with "wild children," youngsters who were discovered beyond society and were assumed to have been brought up by wolves. (At some time, we can all recognize our own children somewhere in that scenario.)

Eventually, all children learn the correct ways of being that we call manners. These are, of course, highly variable, shifting from family to family, nation to nation. Stories of bizarre table customs form some of travelers' most exotic souvenirs. In present-day China, for example, public spitting is acceptable, but public nose blowing is not. In our society, spitting is limited to a very small subset of tobacco chewers; otherwise, it is considered rude, if not downright unhealthy. Public sniffing is likewise frowned upon. If a child sniffs, a parent shows up with a tissue, urging the child to blow. Such behavior disgusts the Japanese, who consider public nose blowing taboo. But for them sniffing, even energetically, is seen as laudable, because it signals that the sniffer is exercising self-control.

Differences between families can be smaller, but just as significant. The child who eats supper at her best friend's house can be flummoxed by a very small shift: reciting grace if that is not done at home; being expected to finish everything on her plate if her family has a different attitude; even a different level of clanking and clinking and conversational noise.

During my child-rearing years, two back-to-back incidents showed me where I stood on the continuum of my small social subset. I also learned the surprising intensity of feeling occasioned by differences that, in the scheme of things, were not very large. Once, during a holiday time, we ate at a nice restaurant with another family. One of their kids got bored, left the table, and sat down in the middle of the stairs that led to an adjoining room. The girl, who was around ten, took off her shoes and socks and began picking out the lint from between her toes. Her parents, who were vaguely aware of what she was up to, did nothing. To this day, my family recounts this story, making appropriate *eeeeeyyyyyuuu* sounds.

Another time, during those same elementary school years, a different family was visiting us one summer day. We ate supper together on the patio of a very informal restaurant in our minuscule downtown. Service was awful; this time all the kids were bored. (The other family had a couple of school-age kids as well as a little boy, about three or four.) I told the kids they could all go to the adjoining playground for a few minutes; I would give them a wave when our dinner arrived. But when the other mother realized what I had done, she was as aghast at my poor manners as I had been at the toe incident a few months before. For all I know, that family may still be saying *eeeeeyuuuu* about us.

Every time we sit down together, we arrive at a consensus for what manners are acceptable at that meal. Sometimes it is spoken: *Oh, go on; pick it up with your fingers.* Or, *Don't bother to wait for me. Go ahead and eat before your food gets cold.* Sometimes it is only implied. Kids eat differently in a school cafeteria than they do when their grandmother takes them for a special outing. If we are anxious to make a good impression, we carefully monitor our behavior at a formal business dinner, or at a meal with the family of a sweetheart we are trying to impress. When it's Chinese take-out at home, some families grab food from the paper containers, while others put the chop suey in proper serving bowls. Eating shellfish requires a different standard — using mallets and crackers to break the shells, wearing big napkins like babies.

Sharing a meal means that we have agreed, implicitly, to eat in the same place at the same time. We have decided to be hungry together. We all eat more or less the same thing. And we try to be pleasant, or at least cordial, to each other. (We hope!)

In manners as in so many other domains, the military has its own way of doing things. One of my friend Mike's strongest memories of his army basic training was of eating lunch standing up. The idea was to be ready for action at all times. Any soldier who tried to sit down could count on being severely reprimanded. Breakfast also conveyed a military lesson, this one about the value of physical conditioning and seamless group functioning. In order to reach his meal, each soldier was required to proceed hand over hand across a set of parallel bars at a pace designed to not bump into the person in front of him and not be overtaken by the person behind him. Physical fitness or manners? I'd say a bit of both.

At West Point, where uniformity of behavior is an important goal, cadets eat rigidly controlled portions and have a carefully limited period of time in which to eat. The practice of eating "square meals" (lifting each forkful straight up and then across) has been discontinued, but mealtime is still an occasion for promoting strict adherence to group norms.

In our family groups, manners promote a sense of well-being and caring. (Our families are not normally fighting units.) We think of the others, we don't take more than our share. Adults help children by cutting their meat, or by serving out their food. Infants, or the infirm, are spoon-fed, a phrase that is so apt, we use it beyond the table.

Children must learn to control their bodies — no squirming, spitting, scratching, hitting, tickling, fist pounding, or drumming. They must sit upright and maintain a distance from other diners. (We are not medieval; we are modern!) They must use cutlery and handle food in keeping with their social set or the occasion. (I am capable of eating watermelon either with a knife and fork or with my hands. I have to know when to do which.)

Through the mini lessons of table manners, children learn to share, to think of others. By saying please and thank you, we recognize the humanity of our tablemate, acknowledging the fact that we both deserve a bit of respect. When we thank the cook, we address the fact that it has taken him some effort to produce the hamburger we are about to eat.

You may not have the best table manners in the world, but you (along with your spouse or partner) are the manners expert in your house, doling out judgments about what is expected, what is permissible, what is beyond the pale.

In my house, because I am almost always the cook, the rule is that the cook can choose what she wants to make. (I do take requests.) My kids were given what were called no-thank-you helpings. The name was taken from a summer camp I had attended; there, when the serving dish was passed to you, you had a choice of saying either *Yes please* or *No thank you*. The *No thank you* would get you a small taste of something you didn't necessarily like, but were expected to try. It seemed liked a reasonable approach to me, so I instituted it for my kids. However, I rarely insisted that they actually taste the food; just having it on their plate seemed like enough.

In addition to letting you know how strict I was as a parent, this also illustrates how mealtimes take on layers of meaning. When I explained the no-thank-you helping to my husband and kids, it brought my own childhood to our kitchen table; the long wooden camp tables filled with friends entered our lives.

If I didn't force my kids to eat things, I did make them clear the table. In my mind, this let them understand that I had worked to come up with the meal, and that I expected them, in some way, to chip in.

Manners are tiny set pieces, often illustrating power relationships. We find the medieval system of display eating bizarre. In our democratic society, we count it impolite to eat in front of another person without offering him something. But if we are paying that person — to fix our sink, say, or our computer — we sit down to our meal without offering him a bite. In our world, cash trumps caste. We learn our little performances, and we teach them to our children. They are mini morality plays, and we know the lines by heart.

WHY A RESTAURANT IS NOT LIKE HOME

Before I call down the wrath of the restaurant gods, let me say that I love eating out, and I do it a lot. I know that having someone else prepare, serve, and clean up is a godsend. But the restaurant industry does not need another champion. The eating-at-home-with-your-family "industry" does.

No matter where restaurants fall on the economic, ethnic, or formality scale — whether they are hosed-down franchises or cloth-napkin establishments — they are all based on an important contradiction: They are at the same time public and private. We lift our little group out of its native habitat and plunk it down in a spot where it is on view. Which is all fine, except that we keep up the pretense that we are still only eating among ourselves. We look (mostly) at each other. We act (more or less) informally. But we are aware of the other groups of diners, who are themselves maintaining the fiction that nobody else around them exists.

We do not speak, or even make eye contact, with the other patrons. Although we may hear every word of the conversation of the people at the next table, we pretend that we don't. And the opposite is true as well. We may act like we are having an intimate little tête-à-tête, but we are in full view, often in full sound range, of a roomful of strangers. It's even more stylized when we meet other folks we know. We nod, or walk over to their table and say hello, but then return to our own group and have nothing further to do with them. The whole enterprise is almost a parody of intimacy, a bit like undressing in front of a window that faces the street.

And then there's the staff. We speak to them in codified ways. That's why all the jokes about knowing the name of our waitperson: We don't really want that person to have an identity beyond that of server. If we are eating in a chain establishment, we can be certain that every word spoken by the person behind the counter has been scripted, much as her civilian clothing has been replaced by a uniform.

The fact that, for diners as well as staff, the dining-out experience is formalized is both good and bad. For families who are pulled in all directions and who, when they do eat at home, cannot free themselves of distractions, the forced togetherness, the limited options, allow them to have the "face time" they cannot otherwise manage.

As the family unit moves out into the world, behavior generally improves. Kids have a chance to put their manners on display (or maybe it just gives parents a goal and a new set of prods). Especially for the parents of small children, being out in public forces everyone to sit still and just *be* together; no jumping up to get a toy or to wipe up a spill. The downside, of course, is that little kids can't sustain this sitting still for very long, so the whole affair gets truncated.

Adults' manners improve as well, and this goes deeper than not slurping or grabbing. Human relations can, for the moment, actually ameliorate. It's rare to have a real blowout in public. Withering tirades, drunken rages, sullen silences, angry ultimatums are not likely to take place where everyone can witness them (see above). We also have a more positive attitude from the get-go: We're spending the money, dammit, and we're going to have a good time. People who have memories of really awful family meals mostly locate those lousy experiences at home. Being out in public is safer; you're on neutral ground. If you want to introduce a loaded topic, or that special someone, to the family, but you don't trust how your clan is going to react, a restaurant meal is much cleaner. It's nobody's turf. Nobody feels relaxed enough to act really badly. Nobody feels at home.

Which is precisely the downside of the experience: Nobody feels at home. It's a social group whose only entrance requirement is the price of the check. No one has actually invited you. No one can kick off her shoes and really relax. You can't run and get the family photo that illustrates the point you are making. You can't decide that you're having such a good time, you'd like to move the after-dinner talk into the living room. In a public setting, no matter how cozy the decor, no matter how well we have dined or how much we have drunk, we are still in a commercial public establishment, with all the space, time, and behavior restrictions that implies.

The brilliantly inventive food writer M. F. K. Fisher tells a story about the time that she worked in Hollywood as a screenwriter during the 1940s. She had been looking forward to cooking a meal for her boss, a studio type she describes only as a Very Important Person. But, she says, "I was tipped off with elaborate tact by his wife, his secretary, and the secretary of his immediate superior in the studio, that he felt bad, in fact terrible, that I had not 'entertained' him." In his world, "entertaining" meant taking him out to dinner.

Fisher takes great pains to arrange the meal ahead of time, finding out her guest's preferences, and then, the day before the event, visiting the restaurant, ordering a menu for the four diners, arranging for the bill to be sent to her house, even leaving a tip in advance. "When I walked out of the restaurant I felt that I had done everything I could to assure my friend of a meal which I could have given him for one-fourth the cost and about one-eighth the bother at home, but which he would, because of his peculiar importance in a very peculiar industry, enjoy a hundred times as much because it was in this peculiar town's smartest eating place."

The next evening, the meal goes splendidly. Her guest is even extremely moved. "Do you know, in my whole life nobody has ever ordered a meal just for me?. . . I hate menus and having to order and — do you know, this is just like a party!"

From Fisher's point of view, the evening "had about it something, no matter how faint, of the festive ease, the latent excitement, of my childhood celebrations — a reward to me for having observed the basic principles of decent dining out. I had treated my guest as much as possible as if he were in my home, and 'miracles occurred.'" She has managed to fulfill his personal needs on a public stage.

For this person, some of his needs were specifically for public recognition. But we all have some variation on those needs. When we eat out, we want to be transformed into a more glamorous, more polished version of ourselves. Even if we are only eating in our local fast-food joint, we want to look like the happy families we see in the ads.

The anthropologist Joanne Finkelstein calls the restaurant a diorama. "We can give a performance as an ardent lover, benevolent friend, generous parent, appreciative spouse or exciting companion. It is an arena in which the fake is not disclosed and honesty is not necessary."

Why has it become a cultural staple to propose marriage over dessert at a favorite, or at least a fancy, restaurant? Is it because, in a public setting, the woman is less likely to say no or make some kind of embarrassing fuss? Is that first scene of formal couplehood an implicit promise of the way their lives together will unfold — in elegant, impersonal splendor? Maybe the juxtaposition of intimacy and exposure adds a frisson.

Another convention — success marked by having the maître d' know your name. (This is a popular shorthand in soap operas.) But do we really want the maître d' to know much more about us? It's an abstraction of human relationships; there's no give-and-take. Let's be honest: You are paying for him to be nice to you.

Still, the dilemma of restaurants is that, in addition to looking for recognition, we are also looking for comfort, especially at the end of a long day. We want to relax. We know we can't put up our feet or let down our hair down in public, but we do crave a level of physical ease. Restaurateurs understand this. They want us to feel cozy and separate — hence the enduring popularity of booths, the preference for corner tables, for banquettes against the wall. These arrangements provide boundaries so that we aren't totally on display, adrift in a sea of strangers. Folks who design restaurants make sure that the lighting is flattering, or at least dim (except for fast-food places, which are utilitarian, but soft). They want us to feel special, fashionable, part of something exciting that's larger than ourselves, hence the popularity of theme menus, food, and decor. Let's be world travelers for a couple of hours.

Or let's at least be part of the vision of a great multinational corporation.

I have heard about a very expensive restaurant in London where your party first enjoys cocktails in a small private room, then progresses to dinner where the first course has been laid out prior to your arrival. Once your group sits down, the table is surrounded by screens. The wait staff peeks in to serve you; otherwise you get something closer to the privacy you would have at home. In general, that just-us-ness is a function of cash. Restaurant owners carefully measure the space between tables. The bigger the check, the more space between you and your neighbor. But nobody wants to eat in an empty restaurant. Aside from making us question the quality of the establishment, we crave the background sense of other diners, even if we don't actually want their company.

Restaurant food can be better and worse than food at home. The preparation may well be more sophisticated, the ingredients more specialized than we are able to handle in our own kitchens. We are becoming more cosmopolitan eaters, even as our cooking skills decline. When it comes to nutrition, though, restaurant meals are no bargain. The 2003 figures from The NPD Group, the leading chronicler of the food industry, for fruit and vegetable consumption give us a snapshot. One point six percent of restaurant dinners include fruit, while 8.6 percent of at-home dinners do. If you factor in vegetables, not counting potatoes or salads, 7.8 percent of restaurant meals include them. However, we eat five times that many vegetables (37 percent) when we eat at home. At the other nutritional extreme, restaurant kitchens go through butter in quantities that would make a home cook gag because, as longtime restaurant professional Anna Kovel explains, "That's how you get the results that people can't get at home. If you want sizzling, crispy potatoes, or one of those great sauces, you have to use a lot of butter."

Although serious high-end chefs are likely to be demanding and sophisticated in their tastes, seeking out fresh ingredients, their goal is to dazzle and to delight. When they put a plate together, their first thought is not nutrition. A main dish generally calls for a protein, a starch, and a vegetable, but professionals are more likely to strike a balance of looks, flavors, textures, and temperatures than worry about nutritional imperatives.

Kids, in particular, do not eat as well when they eat out, especially when you consider that seven out of ten meals eaten in commercial establishments are consumed at fast-food outlets, and that kids are more likely than adults to be fast-food consumers. No matter what kind of restaurant, though, children learn to take advantage of the public situation. They know that the rules may not be as firm as they are at home. There are more variables and, again, in public, parents are reluctant to provoke a scene.

We are more likely to give ourselves treats as well, paying less attention to nutrition than we do in our home routine. And that only takes into account our conscious choices. We really have no idea what goes on in the kitchen. Restaurants are not in business to worry about our health. Those little heart designations on certain menu items came about through public pressure. Desserts, sodas, and alcoholic drinks are profit centers. Drizzling butter or oil on top of a dish before sending it out to the dining room gives it more mouth appeal. By now we all know the correlation between enormous portion sizes and our epidemic of obesity. But it's hard to say no to that image of abundance. And food professionals know that.

Some restaurants feature "family style" eating: At Carmine's, on New York's Upper West Side, diners order huge bowls, which are then shared. At Boston's venerable Durgin Park, patrons are seated at long tables, where they are joined by other parties and served by waitresses whose reputation for high-handedness goes back a century. This familiarity is a big tourist draw. At the other end of the spectrum, a stylish new restaurant in downtown Boston has installed what it calls "the family table," a long table located inside the open kitchen. Being right in the center of the action is popular; people ask for this "kitchen" table when they make reservations.

Perhaps because I have put in a good many years as a home cook, when I go out the last thing I want to see is the work and mess that go into preparing a meal. I think our current mania for display kitchens speaks more to the fact that cooking has become a spectator sport. Go ahead; call me ungrateful. I am backed up by Franco Romagnoli, a Boston institution who has been a TV chef, cookbook author, and restaurant owner. Of the open kitchen, he says, "No matter how trained and good they [the cooks] are, you're looking at how many hands are going into your dish. The theory was, *Look at us, it's pure, uncontaminated.* Instead, I feel the other way 'round." He reminds me, *sotto voce,* "What is done in view is the final cooking. What is done in prep is down in the cellar." And nobody wants to see what happens down there.

In another cultural breakthrough, a large new red-sauce Italian place next to a major highway near me has a startling addition. In the room where the huge bar is located, not only are there TVs playing above the liquor bottles, but the booths along the side of the room feature small TVs, much like juke-boxes. So if you want a really homelike experience, you can watch TV with your family instead of talking to them.

If you're feeling negative, you could say that the subtext of these kinds of innovations is that people are afraid of family life, where relationships get negotiated, where something untoward, something unauthorized, might pop out. They want to create the illusion of intimacy without its attendant risks. The restaurant neutralizes tensions, puts a good face on things. Being in public is a very safe, bounded way to "do" family.

And yet, when we eat out, what we crave is the social experience. A recent study by a team of British scholars found that the most common complaints about restaurant meals were not about price or food, but about whether everyone's meal showed up at the same time. "This appeared to be the most disconcerting of potential technical errors and probably underlines the persistence of rituals associated with the injunction that no-one should start eating before all are provided for," say the authors, Alan Warde and Lydia Martens. "It is probably a more grave mistake than selling unappetising food, suggesting thereby that the satisfactions derived from the social rituals of companionship — eating *together* — outweigh those of the food itself."

For families as well as for nonfamilial groups, in the space of a generation restaurants have moved from occasional treat to mainstay. Paradoxically, taking away the food-preparation "job" from the family also removes one more pillar of support. Few things in life have as much emotional resonance as feeding. In most human societies, food has been provided in a framework of social obligation, with responsibility for feeding our children, our relatives, and, in some cultures, neighbors and travelers as well. When we remove eating from the home, we weaken the bonds of affection and duty. By going to restaurants, we still provide food for our young, but in a more abstract way. When our children grow, will their strongest emotional memories of nourishment come from Ronald McDonald?

In addition, the line between restaurant and home is blurring. According to Harry Balzer of The NPD Group, the number of people eating out is flat. The large growth in the restaurant business in recent years has been in take-out. We have now passed some sort of watershed: Half of all restaurant-produced meals are taken out. We bring prepared foods to the workplace, to the athletic event, to the family reunion. And, yes, of course, to the home.

Also, let's not forget that, in most instances, eating out will cost you more. Although commercial establishments use economies of scale (it's cheaper to buy eggs by the gross than by the dozen), customers are still paying for labor, rent, insurance, utilities, advertising. The rule of thumb I have heard from both food professionals and statisticians is that food costs account for only between a quarter and a third of your restaurant bill. Balzer explains, "When you go to a restaurant, for the most part you're not paying for food; you're paying for service." If you are really interested in saving money, you would do much better to improve your cooking skills.

Again, I am not saying that restaurants are bad. For the family, eating out together can remove distractions. If you are a poor cook, the food that you eat out will be better prepared. And I don't want to diminish for a second the pleasure of having someone do the shopping, cook your food, set your table, bring you your meal, and take it away when you're finished, whisking the dirty dishes off to the kitchen and out of sight. Not to mention that it sure can be nice to get out of the house.

Still, we should think about why, in our current cultural climate, restaurants connote leisure, while eating at home connotes work. I would argue that, if you are in the habit of cooking and eating together, then preparing good things to be enjoyed by the people you care about can satisfy in a very deep way. Because feeding is the most basic animal form of caring, sharing meals is one of the most central familial bonds. When we take our meals in restaurants, we abdicate that function, outsourcing it; moving it offshore. It has to have a weakening effect.

So please, by all means, enjoy your restaurant meal. But be aware of what you are giving up when you hand over the food preparation and service to strangers. As the wonderful writer Laurie Colwin said, "The table is a meeting place, a gathering ground, the source of sustenance and nourishment, festivity, safety and satisfaction. A person cooking is a person giving: Even the simplest food is a gift."

— 5 —

Nourishment

KIDS IN THE KITCHEN

WHEN I WAS in my early twenties, first living on my own, this is how I figured out how to cook: I would think about what I wanted to make, and then I would imagine my mother's pots and pans. Breaded veal cutlets? The big frying pan with the uneven bottom had to be filled a quarter of the way with strained, saved oil. (I could picture the bottle she stored it in.) Meatballs were mixed in the faded red-orange Pyrex nesting bowl. (The egg was beaten in there first.) By picturing my mother going through each step, I could conjure up how to make any dish. For baking, or for serious soups, I had to imagine my grandmother's older, more dented pans and her blue-and-tan earthenware bowls. During my childhood, girls were expected to spend a lot of time in the kitchen. Luckily, I always loved it. Cooking was tactile, it was a real adult job, and it resulted in good things to eat.

When my own kids were small, they were in the kitchen because that's where I was. (Good feminist that I was, I was careful to involve both my son and my daughter.) At first, the kids did the sort of "cooking" that involves banging pots and pans on the floor, or helping out by "washing the dishes" —

playing with plastic containers in the sink while I got something done. Over the years, their interest in cooking waxed and waned. But when they decided they wanted to make something, they had enough knowledge and confidence to give them a head start.

The prevailing wisdom nowadays is that, apart from gourmet fanatics, only a chump would waste time in the kitchen. We are encouraged to spend a king's ransom on appliances, but to actually position ourselves at those space-age counters is most often presented as being either demeaning or just plain absurd. Who has time to cook anymore? What kind of drudge would want to stand over the sink all day producing vegetable peels? Don't we have much more exciting things to do?

Here is the problem: The less we know about how to put together a meal, even a very simple one, the more daunting it becomes. If we are not comfortable in the kitchen, every time we enter it, it becomes a big deal. A steady diet of restaurant or fast-food dinners — even watching too many TV cooking shows — distances us from our own modest efforts. If we measure ourselves against professionals, the standards will be impossibly high. Eventually, if not sooner, the kitchen becomes terra incognito, a place to pass through on the way to the car.

There is no need to become an obsessive chef, but rather what used to be known as a good home cook — someone who has a few standard dishes she can turn out without breaking a sweat; someone who knows enough about how food operates to expand her repertoire, but only if and when she wants. Today, the job is no longer gender specific, which is all to the good. Still, one thing we seem to have lost along the way toward equality is the sense that children belong in the kitchen. It is a wonderful place for them to hang out, to play, to participate, to learn. Food is irresistible. Food prep is tactile, everyday magic. Cooking is something you can do together, routinely, without making a big deal over it. You can talk if you want. Your kids will learn real skills. You will end up having produced a meal.

I'd like you to meet two women who helped me understand more about just how well kitchens and kids combine.

For Lynn Fredericks, it started with basil. She was an overworked single mom with two sons, one still in diapers. Supper consisted of her dragging the kids away from the TV in the living room to sit in front of the TV in the kitchen. While she fed them, she picked at her own food, walked around the room, or else talked on the phone. She knew that something was wrong with the way that her family dinnertime had imploded, but she had no idea of how or what to change.

Then, one night, in desperation, she handed her bored one-year-old a bunch of basil and told him to rip the leaves off. She explained that he could help her cook. Her son's competence at the job, coupled with his joy at having completed what was obviously a useful task, made it a lightbulb moment for Fredericks. Maybe supper wouldn't always be a dead spot in her day. Maybe, instead of pushing the kids away, she could turn this into a time that could bring them closer. To hear her tell it, when she was mired in her postdivorce gloom, the basil was the first step on a path of profound family change.

Instead of focusing on how quickly she could get the meal onto the table because the kids were starving and she had so many things she had to get done, Fredericks began to pay attention to the process of putting the meal together, and including her kids. Little by little, she gave them tasks that they could accomplish, praising them profusely for their success. She relaxed her standards of neatness in the kitchen. (She repeats this often, so neat freaks, take heed. Kids need to learn about cleaning up as they go, but parents and kids both need to know that accidents are part of life.) She made sure the boys had tools that were the right size for them, and she made sure they knew how to use them. Individually and together, they took pride in their work. Most important, she and her kids began enjoying themselves, and each other.

The ripples widened. Fredericks noticed that if the children were involved in preparing the meal, their hunger pangs eased; they didn't have to be fed right away. Once their egos and skills were involved, they stopped rejecting foods out of hand. Broccoli was no longer the only vegetable they would accept. They still didn't like everything, but they became much more willing to taste different foods. When she let them choose menus and ingredients, she was surprised at their adventurousness and creativity. She began taking them to the supermarket, and to farmer's markets — real eye openers for city kids.

But there were always real-world limits. Although she let her boys take turns choosing foods they wanted to cook, she kept them on a budget. There were also time constraints. Fredericks was working. She was not exactly spending her days doing prep work for her sons' star appearances at suppertime. Still, the success of the project was more than she ever imagined.

In time, Fredericks shut off the TV, then moved supper into the dining room. She says that, when she introduced table linens and cloth napkins (each person keeping his napkin for a week), conversation improved. Also important, she says, they began saying a short "blessing" before dinner, with each person saying what he was grateful for that particular day. She writes, "I would not be exaggerating if I stated that this was the last bit of glue that mended our broken family. To my great surprise, the children took this aspect of the blessing very seriously and continue to astound me with their offerings. Parents can learn a great deal about their children from their value judgments about what's important to them on a daily basis."

When she clicks off the skills her sons learned in the kitchen, she includes math, chemistry, a sense of responsibility, learning to follow directions, and learning to work as a team. For her older son, especially, who was seven when the project started, cooking became linked with foreign people and lands. He started to ask, "What culture are we cooking tonight?" And she is sure that the confidence he learned through his cooking helped him through some difficult patches at school.

Fredericks notes that, for boys especially, talking can be easier when they are doing something. "It may be impossible to persuade little Stephan to sing me a song he's learned in school. Yet earning my praise over some cooking skill as we work together on the evening meal can prompt him to jump off the step stool and perform the very song I could not drag out of him earlier."

Years have now passed. Fredericks's younger son will soon be a teenager, and her elder son is looking at the end of his teenage years. Like any veteran parent, she is realistic: "Spending time in the kitchen with their mother is not where they want to be." But, she adds, "That's fine. Meals and mealtimes are still important to them. We still have the connection over the meal." And having a solid background in cooking has given them many skills, not the least of which is the ability to put a meal together. "They still do things for themselves," she says, a big plus when you're living with teenage boys. Cooking together gave the Fredericks family a lot more than food.

When I hear that Rosalie Harrington is teaching a family cooking class, kids and parents together, at our local community center, I am overjoyed. For twenty years, Harrington had run a really delightful restaurant in a redbrick nineteenth-century former toy factory. It managed to be, at the same time, special-occasion fancy and utterly comfy and welcoming. Now that she has closed the restaurant, she is teaching.

I show up for the second of four classes. Harrington has close-cropped gray hair and projects a calm efficiency. As I hear about her life and work, she strikes me as a congenitally creative person. She is also extremely close to her Italian roots. I love the way she pronounces marinara: *mah-ree-NAAH-ruh*.

She fills me in on what she has covered in class number one (held from six to eight on a weeknight, supper included). When she tells me the number of things the group prepared the previous week, I am skeptical about how they could have produced them all. But when she explains how she did it, it begins to sound more plausible: Her magic words, repeated often, are: *prep, Baggies, more, freezer,* and *fun.*

She counsels that, because the prep time and the cleanup time aren't much different if you make a little or a lot, you might as well prepare more than you need and put the extra food, in serving-sized portions, into plastic bags destined for freezer or fridge. Then, the next time you need something, you're all ready.

Also, after years of running a restaurant, Harrington stresses the value of preparation, having all of your ingredients out and available before you begin. And technique is important. Learn how to peel, cut, measure, and clean up.

Describing the first week's class, she says, "First I showed them the recipe for my grandmother's meatballs. Instead of doing a pound of pork and beef, you use three pounds. Plus flat-leafed parsley, pine nuts, raisins. You do a whole lot. You have all your options."

The group made tiny meatballs that could go into something she called *wedding soup*, larger ones that could be served with tomato sauce and pasta, and even a cocktail version. Variations included meat loaf and stuffed peppers. "I showed them how to make a quick marinara sauce that's faster than opening up a can, and doesn't have any of the things in it that are bad for you."

On the night that I join the group, Harrington is featuring corn and tomatoes, which are in season, cheap, and fresh. Throughout, she listens to the kids (five girls and one boy, aged five to "almost nine"), asks them questions, keeps them interested.

We start with corn fritters. Harrington has one kid slice the corn from a cob while the cob stands upright in a bowl, so the kernels don't go flying. The week before, she taught the kids how to cut with two hands, making a fist with the hand that steadied the thing being cut, so their fingers stayed away from the knife blade.

The fritter batter is simple: a cup of beer, a cup of flour, a handful of corn. She talks about variations: curry for spice, or sweet fritters that use apples or berries instead of corn. She offers a dipping sauce of about two-thirds low-fat mayonnaise and one-third mustard.

Then it's on to corn chowder. We add red bliss potatoes, which only have to be cut up, not peeled. Corn is thrown in at the end, so it stays crisp; she uses milk, not cream. I watch a little boy very carefully cut a potato in half with a table knife. Then he places the potato cut-side down so it is flat on the board for the next cut. When the adults start exchanging looks like, *Wouldn't it be easier with a real knife?* Harrington tells them that, once they feel confident about how their kids handle a dull knife, they can move them up to a sharp one.

While the chowder is cooking, Harrington puts together a pizza using prebought dough and preshredded mozzarella and Parmesan. Seeing this authentically Italian cook take shortcuts is liberating. She has also slow-roasted a pan of tomatoes in advance. Now she has the kids smoosh the cooked tomatoes, and then place them on the pizza; they love that part. She talks to the kids seriously and respectfully about options. They stay engaged enough that, when the commuter train rumbles through (it stops about ten feet from the building), nobody even looks up — although later on they do take a break to run outside and look up in the night sky and pick out Mars.

Harrington has the kids throw a couple of handfuls of corn on the pizza before it is baked. The kids love the mix of colors; the adults like the fact that they managed to slip in a few more veggies.

Next comes an updated eggplant Parmesan. Harrington previously peeled and sliced an eggplant, then baked the slices with a drizzle of olive oil. The kids layer the slices with the slow-baked tomatoes and the cheeses. As a final touch,

Harrington produces what will become molasses cookies. She put the dough together beforehand; the kids roll it into balls, dip the balls in sugar, top each one with a raisin. Harrington whisks them into the oven.

Then we all sit around, eating our delicious meal and chatting about this and that. In the two hours we have been here, we have done a serious amount of cooking and enjoyed a very pleasant, sociable supper. If all this cooking and eating had taken place in a family, the evening would have ended with a well-stocked freezer as well as a feeling of satisfaction.

The families at the class already make a point of trying to eat together; the new ingredient is including their kids in the cooking. They talk about friends of theirs who don't bother with supper at all, who seem almost proud that their kids have to eat in the car. They describe houses where one parent, usually the mother, prepares a meal but then just sets it out on the counter, and the kids run through and each grab something separately at different times. Most of them talk about how important supper was in their lives when they were children, and how they want their own kids to have the confidence that comes from knowing that the family will get together regularly.

One mother whose daughter's eating habits are extremely limited is happy that her child tasted a morsel of fritter. "I indulge her," she says apologetically, before going on to talk wistfully about a friend of hers whose kids eat blue cheese, clams, everything.

Harrington answers, "Maybe this will be an introduction to other things," and the mother nods seriously. This is one of the mothers who managed to avoid tasting the fritters, I assumed because of the fat. I am reminded of the time when we took our puppy to obedience classes and realized that it was the owners, more than the puppies, who needed to be trained.

Afterward, I sit and talk to Harrington over a glass of wine. She tells me that she grew up in Boston, the grandchild of Italian immigrants. Her family was unusual in that she had a single mom who worked full time. She says that, when she was a girl, her mother would call her from work, tell her to peel the carrots or cook the potatoes so that, when she got home, she would have a head start on supper. When Harrington was the age of the children in the class, she says, she was making pasta by herself.

But she didn't really understand the totality of cooking until her mother remarried. When Harrington was seven or eight, she recalls, she was put on a train by herself and sent to visit her new grandmother in Mississippi. While her mother was very neat and fastidious in the kitchen, the summer Harrison spent with this new kindred spirit was a revelation. "We picked pecans and made pecan pie. She had chickens. We wrung their necks, and then cooked them and ate them. We ate watermelon, and pickled the rind. She made it feel like fun. I didn't have to worry about being too neat. 'Child,' she would say, 'it's only flour.'

"I really *got* it with her. Those peaches came off of a tree. Those pecans came off of a tree. I think, today, we're raising a whole generation that never saw a pie coming out of the oven.

"Food is such an avenue to culture. You can have a theme dinner, make it fun. I saw an exhibition of Frida Kahlo recently in Seattle. It was terrific; I saw so many things I hadn't seen before. You could have a whole Mexican meal. Make tacos. Have all different fillings. It doesn't have to be a birthday; it's a celebration of life; we're all here together."

Indeed, kids learn not just what to do, but also the spirit in which they can do it. That's why, in the kitchen, one of the most important categories of equipment is the chairs.

WHAT EATING PROBLEMS?

Ellyn Satter is a dietician, therapist, and author who helps "normal" parents with "normal" kids. For my money, she could play the child who calls out the news about the emperor and his stylish new duds. You hear her no-nonsense mid-western voice and you wonder, *Why didn't anyone think of this before?* In her books she occasionally prefaces a piece of advice with a quick, "Settle down." For parents who are overwhelmed and undersupported, she is the calm neighbor or wise family member who, these days, is in such short supply.

Here is what she calls the secret of feeding a healthy family: "The parent is responsible for the *what, when,* and *where* of feeding, and the child is responsible for the *how much* and *whether* of eating." This division of responsibility sucks the oxygen right out of any number of eating/feeding fires. It helps set the stage for family meals that are civilized and enjoyable. It goes some distance toward fending off our contemporary plague of disturbed eating, which, in Satter's universe, includes anorexia, bulimia, obesity, and one more — extreme finickiness.

If Satter's insight came in a flash, she spent many years getting to the point where she could see that light. She grew up in a small town where, she says, "The town whistle would go off at six o'clock. Everyone would know to go home for supper." She became "a pretty traditional dietician" specializing in children. Her primary tool was food selection — telling parents which foods were good to eat, which ones were bad. But, she says, "It became increasingly apparent to me in parent after parent, session after session, that it wasn't that simple."

She tells me that the matter came to a head when a mother sought her advice in dealing with an overweight child. "I told her about the four basic food groups (this was a long time ago), and what she should serve him for meals and snacks."

But this mother had been doing all the right things, to no avail. In addition, she had another child at home who was skinny, not fat. She was worried about him, too. Satter reports, "She was just getting madder and madder at me. 'I'm doing it just the way you said. How can I get this one to eat less and that one to eat more?'"

Satter tells me how, out of nowhere, she came up with a piece of advice: "I said, 'It's not up to you to decide how much your children are going to eat. Your job is to put the food on the table. Their job is to eat.' It startled her, and it startled me. I thought, *Holy smokes, where did that come from?* But it was better than anything else I said that day."

Years later, Satter knows a bit more about why her approach works: "It honors the parents with a very real responsibility. It also honors the child's prerogative about their own preferences and tastes; their desire to eat or not to eat." It takes a lot of the burden off parents and helps children become more responsible for their own eating. They learn to listen to their bodies' cues about hunger and satiety. This approach helps disentangle food from other relationship issues.

Satter finds support in clinical studies. The most compelling one tracked 185 San Francisco–area children from age six months to sixteen and a half years. It concluded, in 1991, that, "Fat infants are at no greater risk than thin ones of growing up fat." But it went on to say that the risk of later obesity increased when, in the toddler years, there was a lack of structure in feeding times, or when there was "increased parental concern about obesity."

The lesson? Parents should provide regular, enjoyable, satisfying meals and snacks. And then they should relax. Satter, like other professionals, also urges parents to look to their own eating habits before going after their kids. "Parents who diet have children who diet at an early age. Parents who diet have trouble trusting their children's ability to regulate their eating and develop the body that is right for them. Parents who diet tend to be cranky and tired, and they make less interesting meals than people who take good care of themselves with eating."

I love Satter's approach because she keeps bringing us back to a basic truth — that eating and sharing food are inherently pleasurable. She lets us see how our culture has subverted our enjoyment, surrounding food with a thick web of don'ts.

She worries about our "widespread emphasis on food as medicine and the prevalent, uncomfortable feeling that food is dangerous" — hence our obsession with calories, fat, carbs, salt, or the diet du jour. She also mentions another unfortunate, and prevalent, attitude: "that eating isn't important. In some other countries, people take time for meals, and their meals are gratifying for them. In the United States, eating is something you do in a hurry, or when hunger drives you to it, or when children insist on being fed."

No wonder our children have eating problems! We have taken an activity that is a biological necessity, as well as both a personal and social delight, and turned it into a rulebound sprint. We have replaced a previous generation's rigid laws of etiquette with pronouncements about what is good or bad for us. Satter says, "Our anxiety and inability to manage our own eating makes us overmanage our children's eating, imposing on them our own controlling and withholding feeding methods — our anxiety and avoidance.... Children who are controlled and overmanaged (or, conversely, not given supports or limits) don't learn to be healthy eaters. They learn to take the easy way out — or to fight with their parents rather than taking responsibility for their own eating."

Then factor in our fast-paced world "with no one family member assigned to providing a meal," and you have a recipe for disaster.

Which is why Satter's commonsense approach is such a relief. She tells us to settle down, relax, and enjoy ourselves and each other. She writes, "Whether your family numbers one or ten (a family is what you are when you start taking care of yourself), meals are as essential for nurturing as they are for nutrition. Meals provide us all with reliable access to food, and they provide children with dependable access to their parents and to caring. Without meals, a home is just a place to stay."

When I ask Satter how she thinks we've arrived at our current situation, she first mentions that, in the towns where the six o'clock supper whistle used to blow, schools are now scheduling six o'clock football practice. "The social supports for parents have eroded. These days, parents have to create every darn thing.... I think we're doing a rotten job as a culture with our parents. We do so little to help them."

But she also faults what she calls "the trend to permissive parenting, with parents feeling apologetic about imposing structure and setting limits, especially around food ... I think today's parents don't really know how important they are."

When she talks about how children need structure, and

about how much they appreciate it coming from their parents, I hear echoes of the anti-drug messages from CASA, the National Center on Addiction and Substance Abuse at Columbia University. Satter seems to be urging us to stand up for our right to enjoy our families.

Another of Satter's pet peeves is what you might call the dumbing down of family meals. She knows that children are often reluctant to try new foods, and that it can take a youngster a long time to develop a taste for something. (Remember those Mexican children.) But that is not a reason to put everyone on a toddler diet. And it is not a reason to become a short-order cook.

I have already described the way I handled this with my own kids, giving them no-thank-you helpings. My mother had a different method. She would say, "Why don't you try it? You're older now; your tastes have changed. You might like it." I didn't believe her, but her underlying message was the same — you will grow up and learn to enjoy grown-up food. In time, my sister and I ate pretty much everything our parents did. There were a few notable exceptions, like the specialty Old Country dish my aunt would bring over on occasion, made of the gelatin that came from a cow's hoof. I think the part of my childhood meals that would have earned points with Satter was the way my father would slice into a fresh Jersey tomato sprinkled with salt, or a nice piece of apple pie. He'd look up at us, grin, and say, "This is living!"

Satter insists that part of a child's job is to behave reasonably at the table. I'm with her there. We're talking age appropriate, of course. But nobody's supper is improved by the presence of a small monster. *Honor the cook* is a motto that should hang atop every stove. *Yes please* and *no thanks* can be learned at a pretty young age.

Satter also has a word for constant snacking. She doesn't call it by its contemporary name of grazing, but refers to it as begging. She reminds us that it undermines the purpose of coming to the table. It's the passive-aggressive form of thumbing your nose at the communal assumptions of the shared meal.

Satter says, "Giving in to his [your child's] random begging for food and beverages puts him in charge of the menu (your job) and keeps him from working up enough of an appetite to take an interest in meals (his job)." Although she recommends keeping bread on the table, she is dead set against a parent's becoming a short-order cook. It will leave the adult feeling overburdened and frustrated, and will produce a child who is more finicky, not less.

Perhaps most important: "For your child to join you at the table, you have to have a table for him to join." Satter tells me about two families she's counseling. In one, a little boy was "absolutely food preoccupied. He ate so much at the table, he threw up. The family had erratic mealtimes." Satter advised them to institute regular family mealtimes and, although they were very busy, "they made it a point to have dinners, and they just did. Within two weeks, the child had settled down. He was just a much happier boy. He knew he was going to get fed."

In another family, however, things are not turning around so easily. The mom is a very finicky eater. Because she had been forced to eat as a child, she was determined never to pressure her own kids. But she went too far in the other direction. "She didn't expect anything from her children. She short-order cooked for them constantly. One child is intensely finicky."

Satter advised this woman to first work on structure. Because her kids snack all the time, the first step is to just get everybody to the table. If they're all eating individual foods, then the first goal is for them to do it at the same place and time. She says it will probably take them a month or six weeks to realize that they enjoy eating together. At that point, the mother can think about changing the foods that they eat. "It depends where the family is starting from."

Satter sounds a note I hear again and again, yet which bears repeating: Family supper is important because it gives children reliable access to their parents. It provides anchoring for everyone's day. It emphasizes the importance of the family nonverbally. It reminds the child that the family is there, and that she is part of it. But parents have to keep their expectations realistic. Because of the stepped-up pace of today's world, they are not going to reproduce the suppers they may remember from their own childhood. Still, they can have satisfying suppers that meet their needs today.

Satter has a sort of Zen approach to living in the world, urging parents to take advantage of the richness of our food environment, by which she means making occasional wise use of prepackaged food. And planning ahead. And not living in fear of fat, or salt, or even fast food. An occasional meal at McDonald's is not going to kill you, she says. And it will help your kids learn to make wise choices.

Satter's bottom line? "I do think it's going to take a community effort to turn this thing around." Societal supports are sorely missing. But, she says, "My read is that parents really do want to have family meals."

TEENS, CALORIES, DOLLARS, POUNDS, AND TV

One of the benefits of supper is that it gives us adults an obvious, ongoing forum for discussing nutrition. Or at least letting our kids see what we eat. Not that it's easy being the local authority on this topic when we get such strange messages ourselves. When my parents dropped me off for my freshman year at college, a generation ago, my mother-the-nurse had two parting words: "Eat protein." In the intervening years, a parade of experts has informed me, with unwavering certitude, that my mother was wrong. First I was exhorted to eat less protein and more carbohydrates; then to eat only natural foods and surely no sugar; then pasta pasta pasta (plus complex carbohydrates). The world moved on to less fat, then no fat. Then unrefined foods, Mediterranean; globs of fat but no carbohydrates; until all of a sudden the nutritionally aware people were singing the praises of protein again. We need to be skeptical consumers of information about nutrition. Just as we work to provide our kids with order and consistency in their schedules, we should present generally healthy, tasty meals in an atmosphere conducive to the enjoyment of eating.

Parents are more likely to pay close attention to what goes into their children's mouths while they are little. By the time the kids head off to school, that attention wanders. No matter that nutritionists are always telling us to eat breakfasts like kings, too many youngsters start the day as paupers, gulping down something minimal on the way to the bus or car pool. At midday, school lunchrooms can be noisy, smelly, and socially fraught; the food is often terrible besides, in terms of both nutrition and taste. So kids can fly through their day with little in their stomachs, making them vulnerable to nutritionally negligible after-school snacks. Even if we lovingly pack our kids' lunchboxes, they are free to trade with their friends or just plain not eat. So supper holds out our last, best hope of the day for healthy eating.

Research about family meals and nutrition is just in its infancy. One thing is clear, though: As parents, we are still the biggest influence on the eating habits of our offspring. Family suppers, that time when the clan can assert its authority, can be a significant force for good.

By the time our offspring reach adolescence, however, you hear weary parents of all persuasions intoning their *Don't sweat the small stuff* mantra. Too often, nutrition slides into the small-stuff box. Our cultural model stresses alienation, distance, rebellion, and a notoriously poor diet. It can take something as extreme as anorexia to catch a parent's attention, although I say bravo to the kids who take a principled stand for vegetarianism. They may be inconsistent, shrill, or misinformed, but they are applying their idealism where they live. That said, let us wade into the murky waters of teen nutrition.

I have already mentioned a 1998–99 study at the School of Public Health at the University of Minnesota in connection with teens' behavior and mental states. Now I would like to refer to its findings about nutrition. The five thousand teenagers studied were extremely diverse in ethnicity and class, and researchers found a broad range of expectations around family meals. Fourteen percent of the teens had not eaten a single meal with their family in the previous week, and an additional 19 percent had eaten only one or two. But just under a quarter of the kids had eaten with their family seven or more times. (Keep in mind that the category was meals, not necessarily supper.)

The researchers found that kids who ate more meals with their families ate more "fruits, vegetables, grains, and calcium-rich foods." They also had more protein, iron, folate, fiber, and vitamins A, C, E, and B$_6$. They drank fewer soft drinks. There was little or no difference in the amount of whole dairy products, red meat, or snack foods.

Interestingly, some of the kids were more concerned about nutrition than were their parents. One seventh-grade boy reported, "It's hard to find a piece of fruit at my house." A tenth-grade boy said, "My friends usually eat healthier, 'cause all our parents don't usually eat all healthy stuff. We all know that they're all getting fat from eating all that fat and we're all usually just eating vegetables and good stuff, like meat that's not all fat and soaking in grease." But the alternative to family meals for most kids appears to be fast food.

When I speak to the principal investigator, Dianne Neumark-Sztainer, she is the first to say that we really don't know enough about what kinds of things influence teens. But the kids themselves point to family meals. The Minnesota youngsters were overwhelmingly positive, with three-quarters saying that they enjoyed eating meals with their family. In the initial focus groups, 62 percent agreed with the statement, "In my family, dinnertime is more than just about getting food; it is a time when we all have a chance to talk with each other." But 20 percent agreed with the following: "Mealtime has often been a time when people argue in my family." The choice should be obvious. If you want to feed your kids well, make sure the supper table is an appealing place to be. And don't underestimate your influence and authority. Your adolescent will probably not ask you to institute, regularize, or increase family mealtimes. But that doesn't mean he won't appreciate it.

At the same time, back east in Massachusetts, Matthew Gillman was coming to his study of adolescent nutrition from watching his own family. His three kids were young, he and his wife each worked one night a week, and family supper, while appealing, looked like a moving target. Still, according to Gillman, "We try our very hardest to do family dinners. In fact, part of our kids' allowance is geared toward do they set the table, clear, can they sit at the table for fifteen minutes." But what he calls the domestic challenge of scheduling family meals got him thinking about the nutritional value of eating together as a family.

Gillman, who is a research physician at Harvard Medical School, conceived of a very large survey. In 1996, his team began studying the eating habits of more than sixteen thousand adolescents. They were able to do this because they linked up with the ongoing Nurses' Health Study to interview nurses' children. At the beginning of the survey, these kids were nine through fourteen. There were follow-up studies in 1998, in 2000, and again in 2002. Residents came from all fifty states and several U.S. territories. They studied the kids' diet, activity, and weight changes. And they found that eating supper with their families was "highly related to diet quality as we measured it."

But Gillman is quick to stress the limits of the study. Because it is a self-administered questionnaire, "We didn't get behind the questions, Is what they prepare more nutritious? Is it the conversations around nutrition that allow them to eat better-quality diet when they're away from home?"

Still, the results speak for themselves. Children who ate dinner with their families every day had an average of one more serving of fruit and vegetables than those who did not. Although, across the board, only one-fifth of the youngsters met the national recommendations of at least five servings of fruit and vegetables a day (depressing, when you think that these are the offspring of health professionals), for every increase in one category (say, moving from sharing supper "some days" up to "most days"), kids were 45 percent more likely to meet that goal of five a day.

Other results were similar to those that Neumark-Sztainer found in Minnesota. In addition to eating more fruits and vegetables, kids who ate dinner with their families ate less fried food and soda. They also consumed less saturated and trans fat, and had a decreased glycemic load, which is a measure of the diet's propensity to raise blood glucose. Interestingly, these differences held true even when the children ate outside the home. The researchers think this might be because, when families eat supper together, they discuss nutrition. So these kids would be more aware of what they should or should not be eating no matter where they were.

Another important variable was the change over time. As the children got older, they were less likely to have supper with their parents: More than half of the nine-year-olds ate supper with their family every day, but only about a third of the fourteen-year-olds did. This is a place where families really have to pay attention. Do fourteen-year-olds need the reliable connection that comes from a family meal any less than nine-year-olds do? In a society that grooms children to move out of the nest, it's easy to let that nest fall into disrepair too soon.

The Boston study also showed a noticeable correlation

between family dinners and obesity. Over time, the kids who ate more family dinners had lower BMIs (Body Mass Index). Those who had family dinners "never or some days" had an average BMI of 19.2. Those who had family dinners "every day" had an average BMI of 18.9, a difference of about one-fiftieth of their weight. In a child who weighed a hundred pounds, the difference would thus be about two pounds.

"That's probably not a lot today," Gillman says, "but if you were gaining two pounds per year more than your compatriot who had the same height and weight, in five years, you would have gained ten pounds more. Things add up over time."

In follow-up studies, those kids who ate fewer family dinners gained more weight than those whose level of family dinners stayed the same or increased.

Gillman calls these effects "modest," but says, "They add to our knowledge about the individual and societal determinants of weight gain. I wouldn't want to conclude from this that forcing the mother or father to make dinner for their family is the be-all and end-all to the obesity epidemic. Since we don't really know the mechanisms, I don't think we can leap to conclusions about interventions. However, I think it's enough to give a pat on the back to those families who are eating dinner together. They are doing something good."

And he brings up the cause-or-effect question: "You might not be surprised that, in the same kind of family that is together enough and organized enough to get a meal on the table, the kids have better health habits in general." Still, his conclusion is unequivocal. "Kids who forgo the fast food and soda to eat with their families really do have better-quality diets."

What Babies Know

When I was feeding my young children in 1970s Cambridge, everybody "knew" certain things: That babies had an inherent wisdom. That we were the ones who were screwing them up. That there had even been experiments proving this: Left to their own devices, children would choose a diet that was balanced and healthy, totally good for them. Our job as parents was merely to get out of their way. I had an image of a line of happy babies in identical white bibs and high chairs, stretching out the length of a gym-sized room.

There actually had been such a study, but it was not quite the way I imagined. It took place in the late 1920s and included only thirteen children. The goal of the experiment had little to do with the wisdom of the innocent. Perhaps most significantly, the foods that were offered to those long-ago children bear precious little resemblance to our diet today.

In the early years of the twentieth century, most American babies were breast-fed exclusively for much of their first year. Then, when they began to eat solid foods, they were offered bland, starchy puddings and cereals. The prevailing wisdom was that, in their first years, children couldn't digest meats or vegetables.

Clara Davis, a pediatrician, wasn't sure this was true. She was interested in seeing what would happen if, for their first solid foods, children were given a much greater variety. After a preliminary trial with three infants in Cleveland, she set up an experiment using ten orphans at the Santa Chiara Nursery in Chicago. Babies between six months and a year old who had just been weaned "were allowed to eat what they wanted from a wide range of simple, unmixed foods in whatever quantities they wished," she wrote in a 1930 article for *Parents Magazine*. The foods were not seasoned and did not include butter or sugar.

Also, there were no rows of high chairs. Each baby ate separately, with a nurse at his side. The adult did not offer food or make any comment, but would help the child to eat, if asked. The children were fed three or four regularly scheduled meals a day. Before and after each meal, all foods were carefully weighed. Because the children lived in an institution, their exposure to other foods could be largely controlled.

The correct part of what my friends and I "knew" in the 1970s about the experiment from half a century earlier is that the children ate a wide range of foods. They varied their intake by amount and by choice. They ate unpredictably, going on what the staff called "food jags," the absolute prize going to one child who ate nine eggs at one sitting. (No one else even came close.) Davis reported that the children remained extremely healthy, and were "above the average weights for their heights. . . . Although none are fat infants, all are healthy, vigorous, and active." She assured her audience that they had no digestive problems.

So what, you may wonder, did Davis serve? As she explained it, the experiment was not one of "bringing the baby to the family table and allowing him to eat the pastries, gravies and made dishes commonly found thereon." Oh no. There were thirty-four choices that were rotated, so that each one was available every few days. A dozen choices were offered at each meal. Because of Davis's questions about meat and vegetables, there were plenty of both — bone marrow, bone jelly, liver, kidney, brains, and sweetbreads as well as chicken, lamb, and beef. There were also cabbage, tomatoes, turnips, carrots, spinach, lettuce, potatoes, and cauliflower. There was one fish — haddock. (This was the Midwest, after all, and food was not so easily shipped.) Davis included a variety of cereals — unprocessed whole wheat, Scotch oatmeal, whole barley, yellow cornmeal, and Rykrisp, as well as milk (grade A raw milk, and grade A raw whole lactic milk, by which I think she means buttermilk), eggs, and fruit. The only foods that almost no one liked were sea salt and spinach. Bone marrow, milk, and oatmeal were favorites. (I know that bone marrow is today greeted with disgust, but when I was a child, it was presented as a delicacy, and we relished it; it is soft and sweet.)

Davis intended to follow up with an experiment that included sweetened foods, but the Depression hit and research money dried up. Over the years, her experiment, with the cherubic toddlers and the uniformed nurses, took on a life of its own. As a 1987 article in the *New England Journal of Medicine* commented, "The results of her [Davis's] research have been widely interpreted by health professionals to mean that given a wide variety of choices, children will instinctively select and consume a well-balanced diet. Such a broad conclusion was not drawn by Davis, nor can it be concluded from her research or from any other investigation. Yet, this supposition is frequently stated as fact in medical textbooks and echoed by clinicians. The misinterpretation of Davis' results may lead to an overly relaxed attitude toward poor food habits and contribute to the development of nutritional problems in children."

The article cites more recent research showing that the more variety people are presented with, the more they will eat. (The fact of this variety may have been responsible for a good part of Davis's children's good nutrition. Remember that they were offered a dozen different dishes at each meal.) Today, research about "variety" is more likely to be concerned with the "all you can eat" buffet mentality that has contributed to our obesity epidemic.

Davis herself noted that the mechanism that regulates food intake only functioned on a "primitive diet" such as the one she offered the babies. Although lab rats don't become obese when presented with unlimited lab food, the *New England Journal* article notes that they balloon when given a "supermarket diet" consisting of "chocolate chip cookies, marshmallows, condensed milk, milk chocolate, salami, peanut butter, cheese and bananas."

So Davis's children do have something to teach us, but it is not what we, hanging out at the playground on Cambridge Common, thought. They teach us that, relieved of our adult anxieties and inhibitions, children will be enthusiastic eaters. We can offer all kinds of foods and assume that our kids will like lots of them, if not all of them all the time. We don't have to tie ourselves up in knots worrying about the food preferences of our little darlings, spending our parenting lives as short-order cooks. But we do have to be aware of the nutritional value of food and forgo the "supermarket" diet. Again, it's another reason to eat reasonable, enjoyable, low-key, home-based meals. I just wish you could see the photos of those solid little babies from so long ago.

— 6 —

Spirit and Flesh

GOD COMES TO DINNER

CHRISTIANS MIGHT DO it most demonstratively — *This is my body, this is my blood* — but all spiritual traditions imbue eating with meaning. I've mentioned the Samoans spitting in the food of a relative to transmit strength. Chinese families eat in a tight circle, showing unity and caring. When we put food into our mouths, we are, in some way, admitting the rest of the world into ourselves. When we set this daily act in the context of our belief system, our intake of food affirms our view of the cosmos. Each time we say grace, we are including another presence at our table. Eating consciously, in community, we strengthen our connection to the traditions that sustain us. We are all spirit. We are all flesh.

Bill Huebsch is a Catholic theologian who lives very much in this world. I catch up with him by phone during Holy Week, at the Minnesota farm he shares with his life partner. They raise much of their food, even to the point of growing and slaughtering their own chickens. But Huebsch also does a lot of traveling, promoting a movement called Whole Community Catechesis, aimed at integrating parish, community, teaching, and home life. (*Catechesis* means "oral teaching.") His vision is of a daily life infused with spirituality, and a spiritual life informed by the secular. "We *are* the Church," he has written. "Our homes are where the Church lives every single day."

He was first struck by the power of home meals when he was a graduate student living in a household of Jesuits. They lived very simply, but they made a point of having supper together every night. "They lit a candle, put out a tablecloth. Over supper we would argue all these points of politics, theology, everything."

Now Huebsch tries to help families to likewise see the power of everyday supper. In addition to preparation, cooking, eating, talking, and cleaning up, he urges us to value "lingering over the meal, chatting and allowing each other space to breathe. . . . The events of the day, the supper no matter how simple, and even one's very breath — these are all gifts." His message is that, for families, the supper table is where faith is taught, where it is lived.

Huebsch tells me that "In the Catholic theology, we say that what Christ chose to leave behind as a memorial of himself for his followers was not a theological system or a memorial code. His memorial was a meal — supper — just that." At the Last Supper, he described a new covenant, and told his followers that, when they ate and drank, they would remember him, thus marking a direct and recurring link between eating and faith. Doctrinal wars have been fought over how literally Christians should take the link between bread and body, wine and blood. At the least, however, Christians believe that, when they receive communion, they are ingesting the life and thought and teaching of Jesus. Huebsch explains to me that the centrality of the meal was continued by Jesus' followers. "The Gospel of Luke tells about ten milestones in the life of Christ, and each one takes place at a meal."

If the mass can be seen as a highly evolved meal, then sharing secular supper can be viewed as preparation for taking part in the mass. Huebsch writes, "Anyone whose family regularly shares supper, or Sunday breakfast after Mass, or early coffee before the day begins, can tell you how important this is. Anyone who has lost a spouse to death, or sometimes even to divorce, will tell you that they miss those meals, the shopping they did for them, the cooking, even the cleanup afterward. . . . Even in homes where love has gone cold, where there is a violent or dark temper dominating the household — even there, meals are important. Sometimes those meals explode in rage and sometimes they are times of peace, but they remain important. . . . Things work out when you cook and wash dishes together. It's hard to sit down to table with someone you haven't forgiven."

He tells me, "In most of our lives, meals are also memorials. Almost everyone, when they speak of their lives, they speak about meals." Again, as rituals, they both make and mark transitions. We tend to share them with people who are significant in our lives. And because of our biological makeup (memories are strongly linked with our sense of smell), they form sensual links to our past.

So every time we have supper — regular, profane, everyday supper — it contains echoes of all of the suppers we have had. As well, we sense the echoes of suppers through all the centuries of our faith group. The most ordinary soup and sandwich becomes a powerful piece of living theater.

Huebsch brings it into context for Catholics now. "The way to observe Holy Week is not to spend it on your knees," he tells me, "it's to have supper with people. You're not going to be saved with theology." You're going to be saved by living your faith. For him, that faith is enacted at home.

Another benefit of home meals is their ecumenical nature. Not everyone can receive communion, but anybody can be invited to supper. "The meal focuses people. It brings them together. It suspends distraction for a little while."

Every night that Huebsch isn't traveling, he and his partner share an evening meal, which may be something as simple as a bowl of soup. But that bowl of soup has echoes. He tells me that, the day before, when they were working in the garden, they were talking about what to have for supper. They settled on barbecued chicken wings. Then, he says, "We were remembering other chicken wing events."

Like all of us, Huebsch has overlapping communities. He has his home, his parish, his work helping Guatemalan chicken farmers. For him, there is a very tangible link between food and faith. And he enacts his worldview at supper with family and friends.

"I think at the root of this is a possibility for building a much more tolerant, peaceful society," he says. Supper can be a small spot of peace, fellowship, and sanctity for us all.

My friend Cindy, who was raised in the Catholic church but now is part of an Episcopal parish, calls supper a reminder: "It's that moment in the community, week by week or day by day. Nightly supper is like a liturgy, acting on you in this unconscious way to remind you that the family is important — even if you're fighting. It's a deeply held belief, whether you're conscious of it or not. It's a sharing of community."

She shows me the link between supper and the Episcopal service. First comes the reading of the scripture, which she says is as important as the Eucharist, or communion. Then, after the readings and the sermon, the congregants "eat the meal."

As Cindy explains it, "Jesus said eat it. We eat his words; we eat his meal."

Cindy suggests that I have supper with a young family in her church she describes as living intentionally, and sometimes in community. I am not sure what those terms mean, but one night, when the snow is hardened on the ground, I show up at their mid-nineteenth-century house. The bushes in front are overgrown; the house looks like hasn't been painted in decades. This family, who has recently moved in, has a lot of work ahead of them.

Everyone seems excited to see me: the parents, Paul and Denny; their daughters, Abigail, who is twelve, and Diana, who will be nine in three days; even Sonja, the sleek mutt with one eye. (I am smitten. My dog, Sully, has one eye as well.) We sit right down at their round table (no assigned seats, but personal napkin rings), and Paul asks, "What song shall we start with?"

"Johnny Appleseed!" the girls agree, and everyone joins hands and belts out two enthusiastic verses plus chorus:

> The Lord is good to me
> For this I thank the Lord.
> For giving me the things I need
> The sun, the rain, and the appleseed.
> The Lord is good to me.

Supper is lasagne, salad, plain broccoli, bread and butter. The rule is, if the girls drink two glasses of water, they can have soda. The glasses are small. But once Diana finishes her water and asks for soda, Denny says, "Wouldn't you rather have dessert?" So the rule is evidently soda *or* dessert. That is the extent of the haggling over food.

The girls treat me to reminiscences of their former life in Chicago — their favorite playground, the name of a playmate, a memory of a used-furniture store owned by a family friend. The store had a fire, and for months afterward, those pieces of furniture that didn't get burned were piled up in their dining room.

There is lots of enthusiasm, humor, and shared stories. I learn that Paul has been based at home while Denny holds down a job. He is working toward a master's degree and also rehabbing their house. They are making room for two young couples (one of whom has two small children and a third on the way) who work at the sorts of social service jobs that pay so badly, the couples can barely afford to rent, let alone buy. So room in a rehabbed house will be Paul and Denny's very personal contribution. This is what they mean by living in community now.

When they were first married, it was just the two of them, and neither one could put a meal together. Supper was cheese and crackers, or cereal. Later, when they moved into a community under Quaker auspices, one of the draws was that somebody else would cook. Then, when they moved out on their own again, Denny hired the person who had done the community cooking to teach Paul a few things.

"Menu planning, that's what was hardest for me," he says. "If I had it written down, I could follow it."

Abigail, who has been listening, asks me, "Did you know you could eat applesauce on a fork? My dad does it, so I tried it. You can! When my dad was little, he ate applesauce on spaghetti!" Paul says he doesn't remember this, but his mom has told him that he and his brother went through an applesauce phase, putting it on top of everything. Then Abigail asks him, "Didn't you work in recycling?"

Paul answers her, and Denny asks the girls what they learned in school today. Abigail gives a very cogent explanation of a science lesson about gas and electricity and the northern and southern lights. Diana squirms, makes a face, finally comes up with, "We had Mrs. Rosa. And then we had meeting."

"You like that, don't you?" Denny asks. Her demeanor expresses interest, but she doesn't push.

Denny hands out the girls' vitamins, and the talk turns to people whose hands and feet turn orange from too much vitamin A. Paul looks up vitamin A in the old dictionary they keep nearby. When Denny was growing up, her family kept an encyclopedia next to the table to settle dinner table arguments.

Denny talks about how her father orchestrated dinners. The first time Paul came to supper at their house, her father asked everyone to tell the most boring thing that happened to them that day. "My mother's a very optimistic, positive person," Denny explains. "She thought and thought; she couldn't think of anything. Then Paul said, 'Well, this is the most boring thing that's happened to me.' My father said, 'I wish I had the nerve to say that!' "

This is a story that has obviously been told many times before, but everyone laughs heartily.

By this time we are on to dessert, and Denny asks Diana, who is getting bored, to do something other than wipe each crumb of brownie up with her finger. Diana asks if she can play music. Denny suggests classical; Diana puts in a CD of a Ugandan children's choir. Soon the girls leave the table, and the grown-ups have coffee.

Time flows freely at this table. We are in Chicago, where the girls were born. We are here now, in this old house under construction. We are in the future, when the young families will move in.

I see how supper works to consolidate group identity, shepherding a family through time. Paul's brother, his mom, his dad, his stepmother, even his stepmother's father have put in virtual appearances. Denny's family of origin has shown up, too.

Half a year later, on a warm Indian summer evening, Paul and Denny invite me back. The small room we ate in is now a sitting room. A bright new south-facing room extends the length of the back of the house, overlooking the yard. One end has a little sitting area, as well as a shelf with toddler toys. At the other end, two tables are pushed together, set for supper. Sarah and Andrew, a young married couple, and Chris and Scott, along with their two small boys and brand-new baby, have been living with Paul, Denny, and the girls for about six weeks. There have certainly been a lot of changes, but supper seems calm.

We start off holding hands and singing a beautiful hymn. Sarah has cooked tonight (something called Bulgarian casserole, and salad); the adults take turns preparing the suppers they share on weeknights. Paul has told me that the two boys, aged two and four, graze a lot during the day and don't spend much time at the table. But tonight they seem to do well, and Denny even shows them how to hold a wineglass carefully, with two hands, so they can take a sip of sparkling cider (nonalcoholic, to be sure).

Tonight, Scott is out, because the school where he teaches is having its open house. Alan, a friend of Sarah and Andrew's, has come for supper before the three of them go off to a meeting at church. People sit more or less in family groups, although it's clear that Benny, the four-year-old, enjoys sitting next to nine-year-old Diana, and midway through the meal, Denny takes the baby so Chris can eat.

The talk turns to the suppers of their childhoods. Alan, one of seven boys, remembers it as "a time of joy; rip-roaring laughter." Several remember after-supper Bible readings, with quick sprints through the turgid parts of Leviticus and Deuteronomy. For a couple of weeks over the summer, this group shared singing and prayers after supper, but the practice dwindled. Denny mentions that Sarah would like to start singing together again. This community is still a work in progress.

The three couples know each other from church. Two years ago, when Sarah and Andrew got engaged, they asked Paul and Denny to mentor them. Chris and Scott, in turn, looked after Paul and Denny's girls when their parents were out with the engaged couple. Denny tells me that being with the younger couple set them to remembering the things they had talked about doing someday — building a solar house, renovating an old one. "We just started thinking — what if . . ."

And here is where the "intentional" part comes in. Although Paul and Denny were living in a cape that fit their family of four perfectly well, they decided to buy a house that would be big enough to invite the two young couples to join them for two years. (This would be long enough to work through conflicts, Denny tells me. When they lived in community earlier, people would come for a year, which meant that you could put up with something you didn't like because it would be over soon.)

The idea is for the two young couples to bank their rent money and use it toward a down payment on a house. Before going ahead with the plan, Paul and Denny consulted their parents. Although Denny's dad, an attorney, mentioned that no good deed goes unpunished, they say their parents were encouraging, while the parents of the two younger couples were, according to Denny, "maybe a little amazed.

"But we have the pleasure of little children, of people who have wonderful aesthetic sense. It's a way to have a big family but not pay for college," she offers, half as a joke. They had thought about adopting, but this way the baby comes with parents. Paul and Denny don't have to stay up during the night.

Paul says, "When we started this whole thing, I had an image of a little more structure, a little more house meeting, taking up common spiritual disciplines." But, he adds, "It became clear that I was blowing that horn, and that's all right."

Paul says that one of the benefits of living in community is freedom. The adults can cover for each other. Also, he hopes his daughters will come away with "some sense of generosity. We're counseled to share each other's burdens and to share each other's joys, to live in love with our neighbors. When you bring that inside the home, it just becomes very real and concrete. A lot of the Christian call, though it may not be uniquely so, is how we live together, care for each other." After supper, when he folds up one of the tables, Abigail comes over to help him in a very casual, automatic way.

Right now, supper is the one thing they all share. Paul says it's "really the time that is structured regular time when everyone comes together, both in sociability and in work. Somebody's been working to make that meal. Then somebody has to clean up. It's right there at the center of our being together. It's hard to imagine life without eating together."

Later, my friend Cindy fills me in a bit about communion. "Going to the communion rail is an act of supper, of the community eating together," she says. "There's a wide variety of beliefs about what you're actually eating together, but it's central to the act of worship in the Episcopal church. The community breaks bread together."

Although some Christians believe that, when they receive communion, they are literally eating Jesus' body and blood, for Cindy it's more about "ingesting his laws and whatever he stands for. That's why they call it communion, because it's everyone eating together. In my experience as a Christian, it acts in the same ways as a supper. It contains all the memories of everyone who ever did it.

"Sometimes I do it and just go through the motions," she adds. "Then all of a sudden it strikes me: It's a ritual that works unconsciously in people."

The real eating and the ritual eating are intertwined. Paul's past, and Denny's past, as well as their shared history, are in some sense present at their supper table. The entire community of saints is present when any one of them takes communion. The sacred informs and enriches the mundane. The mundane gives us access to the sacred. It happens in families; it happens in community. Now, in an old house in Massachusetts, a new generation will grow up sharing an old and well-used table. As Cindy would put it, this is their way of eating Christ's word.

BUDDHIST LUNCH

When my friend Sally tells me that she sometimes goes to the Buddhist monastery up the road from her house in Vermont to share in their silent Sunday lunch, I decide that, in the interests of research, I should give it a try. I have never eaten with Buddhists, or with people who weren't talking. I picture a very long table with people nudging each other and pointing toward the soy sauce. I figure there must be a lot of sign language and gesturing.

We go on a sunny day in late April. The daffodils have come out, but the temperatures are still around forty, so if you're outdoors at all, you're aware of the cold.

Here's the deal: Every Sunday, the dozen or so monks who live a couple of towns away come over to this hilltop home of the dozen or so nuns. These folks, whose heads are shaved, and who are dressed in various combinations of brown, make a day of it: dharma talk, walking meditation, silent lunch, more dharma talk. (*Dharma* means "ideal teaching.") The core of the group is Vietnamese, although half the members are Westerners. They welcome visitors on Sundays. Today, there are about two dozen. Most are Americans in various stages of Buddhist-seriousness, as well as one Asian family who has come to visit a relative, one of the nuns. Every once in a while someone rings a bell and we all stop, like kids playing statue. Sally tells me it's to concentrate on what we are doing. Later, I read, it's to enjoy breathing.

Sally and I do the dharma talk (sitting very still in a room, listening to a tape of the group's founder, Thich Nhat Hanh). It is so soothing that I nod off for a second. For the walking meditation, we are to walk normally but focus on our breathing and on the phrase of the day. *Breathe in: I am here for you; breathe out: Mother Earth.* If we prefer, we can substitute the name of a friend, or our name, for *Mother Earth.* We make our way together, maybe thirty of us, along a path through the woods. We stop a couple of times and just look. *No fair,* I think. This is such a gorgeous part of Vermont that just about any place you look is wonderful.

When we get back to the house, one of the nuns sits down outside with the visitors to tell us about the upcoming meal, which they call formal lunch. The food will be served buffet style. The nuns and monks go in order of ordination. (Those who have been there longest go first. We civilians follow.) When we take up our bowls, we are to think about the empty bowls, and be thankful for having something to eat. When we put the food in the bowls, we are to have compassion for all things. We are to take only as much as we can eat. We are to wait until everyone is ready before we begin. A young nun recites a blessing, first in Vietnamese, and then in English:

> This food is the gift of the Earth, the Sky, the
>   Whole Universe and much hard work.
> May we live in such a way as to be worthy to receive it.
> May we transform our unskillful state of mind and
>   learn to eat in moderation.
> May we eat only foods which nourish us and pro-
>   mote good health.
> We accept this food in order to realize the practice
>   of peace and understanding.

The food looks and smells wonderful — brown and white rice, something brown and cut up that must be tofu. A dish made with yellow noodles and veggies (carrots, corn, peas) cut up very very small, and garnished with crushed peanuts. A salad made of cabbage, something slightly gelatinous, and very thin strips of cooked tofu, with three bottles of sauces. The monks and nuns have covered lacquer bowls labeled with their names. Guests can choose bowls or plates; chopsticks, spoon, or fork. Everyone moves very slowly and deliberately, but the line keeps moving.

We file in and sit cross-legged on cushions on the floor, facing each other; female visitors behind the nuns, male visitors behind the monks. We wait. The senior monk hits a bell. People make the bowing namaste sign (my best to you; your best to me). We wait.

After my drive up, and the dharma talk, and the walking meditation, I am really, really ready to eat. The views out the window are gorgeous, but no one looks. Sally is sitting next to me, but I only occasionally sneak a glance at her. Across from me are Vietnamese monks, their faces blank.

Finally, the monks take the covers off their bowls and settle them in their laps, cradling them in their hands. They begin to eat. There is an enormous clatter in the room, and it dawns on me that it is the sound of chewing, accompanied by the scraping of utensils. Amazing! I am listening to forty-odd people chew. It is a surprisingly intimate experience, tuning in to our bodies doing something together.

I am very careful to take one thing at a time, to keep my three courses separate. I lift a forkful very slowly. It is very crunchy. Uh-oh; this is not tofu, it is something very spicy and stringy. What could it possibly be? It is hurting my mouth. And I am supposed to eat it all! How will I do this? I have not had to eat something I didn't want to in years. I have the awful feeling of being a guest in a foreign environment, of having to be polite. I have been very careful to take an amount of food that I will be able to finish, even though I hate doing that. Because, when I was a child, my father always went on about wasting food, I have spent my life always leaving a little bit on my plate, just to show him, no matter that he is long dead. Today I will eat every morsel.

After a while, I decide that the mystery ingredient is ginger marinated in something I can't identify. I have never heard of eating chunks of ginger before, but that is what it is. I mix it with the rice. Luckily, not every piece is equally strong.

Everyone is eating so slowly, I am worrying about how I will draw my food out long enough. I think about what I am eating. Crunch. Peanut. Hint of fennel. Fennel? Fennel. Damned ginger. Blue sky. Glad I chose a fork instead of chopsticks. Although I don't have a problem eating with chopsticks, I figured, why push it.

At a certain point, all the chewing, tasting, becomes boring, then excruciating. How will I make this last long enough? Sally is still eating. One young visitor across from me still has a lot of food on his plate.

Now I realize that someone is finished, and I had better get moving if I want to finish my meal.

The number one monk sets down his bowl, puts the cover on it. Everyone else sets down their bowls. Then he rings a bell. Then he asks the monk next to him to lead a song, which people sing in a lively and happy way: *We are here; it is now. We don't have to worry. We have somewhere to go; something to do; we don't have to hurry.*

We listen to announcements, then all file back into the kitchen and, still in silence, wash our dishes in a series of rectangular plastic basins, then dry them and put them away. Some people take something to drink. I am told that, because Thich Nhat Hanh believes in doing one thing at a time, they don't eat and drink at the same time.

Here is my takeaway: (1) This would be a great weight loss

regimen: chewing each mouthful before you put another one in your mouth, eating slowly, being mindful of your food. Ridiculous thought, Buddhist weight loss plan. (2) This is so much the opposite of the way we eat. Take only what you will eat. Eat only what will help you. Be mindful of what you are eating. Do not do anything else while you eat. Be aware of the others who are with you, but only in a general way. Be mindful of yourself, of what you are doing. Be thankful for the food. Savor each mouthful.

Normally, we shovel our food in, try to do several other things at the same time, eat stuff that we know is junk; eat too much, eat too little; hold out until we can have exactly what we want. So the food-consciousness part of it is terrific. Still, I am sociable enough, or else maybe mired in the world in such an unenlightened way, that I enjoy the give-and-take of talking at meals. Obviously. That is one of the reasons I am writing this book. Insight number three: I am not Buddhist, not by a long shot. Still, it is impressive that forty-some people can eat a meal together with such calm and quiet and ease.

These people have chosen to come to this hilltop, to withdraw from the hurly-burly of the world. They are celibate. They only do one thing at a time; if they are cooking, they will stop what they are doing if they want to talk. But most of us have chosen to live intimately with sexual partners, with children, with parents, with friends. We expect a high degree of intimacy in our households. And so we talk to each other while we eat.

But we can still be mindful of what we are doing, and why we are doing it. For even the most garrulous, driven multi-tasker, home can be a little bit of a windblown hilltop in Vermont.

SKINNED KNEES AT THE TABLE

Although my cousin Zoe lives in Beverly Hills and has a live-in nanny, what strikes me when I visit is that she is managing to raise a couple of unspoiled girls. The twins, at three, are expected to clean up their toys when they are finished; thank their nanny for providing their lunch; treat each other, and the adults they encounter, with respect. They are hardly goody-goodies. They are inquisitive, superactive, laugh-riot toddlers. When I compliment Zoe, she says that everyone at her kids' nursery school is reading something that sounds like *skinned knee*.

I don't catch the full title until I become supper obsessed and begin haunting the Parenting Advice sections of bookstores, where I am overwhelmed by the range of offerings. My own parenting shelf consisted entirely of a hand-me-down edition of Dr. Spock that, luckily, I rarely had to consult. My kids were basically healthy, and I had pretty much instant access to an experienced, commonsensical, if somewhat prickly, old-fashioned doctor — my father. When my son got to be about eight, my father kept insisting that my husband should bring him into the office with him on weekends: "Let him sweep the floor!" my father blustered. I bristled at the gender stereotyping. He expected my daughter to only help me in the kitchen — which she actually loved to do, but that was beside the point. Both kids set and cleared the table at supper, and both argued constantly, unchangingly, for years, about which one did more.

Eventually, I come across the book my cousin mentioned, *The Blessing of a Skinned Knee: Using Jewish Teachings to Raise Self-Reliant Children*. It was the response of a Los Angeles child psychologist, Wendy Mogel, to the question of how to raise capable, responsible, good-humored, self-sufficient youngsters. In her practice, Mogel found herself running out of ideas about how to help well-to-do, well-meaning families ruled by autocratic, unsatisfied, brittle children. At the same time, she began to learn about the Judaism her parents had left behind. She realized that Jewish law and tradition had been parsing the minutiae of human behavior for centuries, and that its approach could help parents like her clients, and like her.

Mogel could see how reframing the familial discussion to include respect, faith, purpose, character, and right living might help parents who were often successful in their professional lives, but who couldn't stop their children from doing thoughtless, obnoxious things like leaving cookie crumbs in the parents' beds. Thinking about their family lives in terms of transcendent values might help beleaguered parents limit the frantic spiral of achieving and doing that was leaving too many children feeling adrift.

On the subject of food, Mogel writes, "In a society without clear and specific moral anchors, many families have turned beliefs about what constitutes a healthy diet into a substitute for religion. By giving moral weight to food choices (low-fat foods and thinness equal virtue, junk food and being overweight equal sin), they substitute food theology for deeper spiritual values." Food should be about "moderation, celebration, and sanctification."

I love Mogel's informed yet commonsense approach. I assume that, because of the book's Jewish core, it would have a limited audience. I can certainly see how it would be a godsend to someone like my cousin.

So I call Mogel to talk to her about supper. I am delighted

to find that, twelve printings later, her book has reached an audience far beyond her population subset. Maybe lots of parents are sick of living in thrall to whiny, demanding kids. Maybe they want someone authoritative to tell them they don't have to feel guilty when they say no. They don't have to become Jewish if they aren't, or even more Jewish if they are. They just have to learn to turn down the volume on the fear-and-anxiety-mongers and listen to the sensible voice inside themselves.

First, Mogel wants to talk about suppertime. Literally, suppertime. She says she no longer recommends that young children wait to eat supper with their parents when they come home from work. The seven-thirty suppertime just doesn't make sense for kids.

"I worked with too many families who came into my office knowing about the correlation between Merit Scholarship winners and eating supper together," she tells me by way of introduction. (Ah yes; the Merit Scholarship connection. I break the news to Mogel that it's a myth.) But the point is that Mogel's clients tend to be conscientious parents who are likely to keep their youngsters up late so they can all eat together.

The cynic in me thinks that at least some of these parents are stopping off at the gym or the bar or the coffee shop on the way home. The caring soul in me asks, And what's wrong with that? Aren't parents entitled to a life beyond family and work?

But Mogel is focused on time: "As much as I want children to have supper with their parents," she says, "I want them to have a good night's sleep."

The parents Mogel sees often feel buffeted by forces they can't control. These are people at the top of many of our societal wish lists, but to them, "It feels like a scarcity economy," which is light-years away from their own childhoods. "For people who grew up in the '50s and '60s, there was a sense of limitless expansion — the country, the economy; the women's movement, civil rights — it seemed like there would be a place for everyone.

"Now everything seems dangerous and conflicted; wildly competitive. . . . The reality is, most of us probably would not get into the colleges we went to."

But parents, peering through their American Dream glasses, still believe that, no matter how successful they themselves are, their children must surpass them. This collision of extraordinarily high expectations, a shifting economy, and an intense identification with their children's accomplishments sets the stage for a grinding, never-good-enough family life.

"Parents are wildly involved in their children's achievement," Mogel says. "They give up time, they give up sleep, they give up real conversation. They give up any sort of downtime."

Mogel has also been consulting to independent schools, which, she says, are caught in a bind: "They talk about having children of character, they talk about children's spiritual lives, but schools are very invested in their placement, in college ranking and SAT scores." After all, that's how they attract more, and more attractive, children.

It's the same bind we're caught in as parents. Nobody wants to create driven automatons, but in our anxiety about individual success we are more likely to err in that direction.

Mogel, however, takes it one step farther: "Again, it's this manic defense against despair, this frenzy that covers a spiritual emptiness."

For Mogel's own family, their new religious ties have helped keep them centered. Shabbat, the Jewish sabbath, has been an anchor. For our purposes, we can think of it as supper writ large — a time to pause, to give thanks, to connect; a regular, recurring gift. Although Mogel's family has not become sabbath observant, they have maintained Shabbat dinner, the family meal that traditionally ushers in the day of rest. Now that her children are teenagers, Mogel says that, for her family, it's as important as it ever was. At their Friday-night suppers, "We still go around the table and say what we're grateful for. They [her children] can see what priorities their parents have. When we light the candles, we light one in the name of anyone who needs a blessing, who may be having a hard time. Then we're done with the sad news . . . There's a Jewish principle — *Joy is legislated on Shabbat*. Once the sabbath candles are lit, we don't have to talk about any problems."

But Mogel realizes that, for families unaccustomed to this type of routine, it can sound stilted. She advises parents who are just trying this out to begin "without a huge agenda of holiness. If just eating take-out food together one night a week is a step forward for you, then that's what you should aim for." She recommends "figuring out what's important for you; what your goals are in raising your children. It's a huge truism: When they're three and five years old, you think it's going to go on forever, but how quickly this happens, they're gone. By the time they're fifteen, you see the end. It takes a tremendous amount of discipline and foresight to protect dinner and family time. If you just follow the flow of the culture . . ." Her voice stops. We both know how easy it is for family time, close connection, to get whittled away.

If you find it hard bucking the tide, Mogel recommends seeking out other parents who share your views, and also talking to parents who have kids slightly older than yours, kids who have turned out okay. This is a simple and powerful piece of advice. If you can find a couple of families you can watch up close, they can be role models for your kids and examples for you. You don't necessarily have to be *like* those parents; they may only show you that a variety of methods can work to produce "successful" kids. That alone may give you the boost you need to do what you instinctively feel is right.

At one point, when my own kids were elementary school age, we began to spend time with a family of cousins whose college-age offspring seemed to be doing very well in life. We wanted to see how their parents had done it. Many years later, I'm not sure we ever got the answer. But we had an awful lot of fun together, with the older cousins really enjoying the younger ones and taking an interest in their progress, which may have been as important, in terms of behavior modeling, as hearing about the impressive schools they were attending.

Still, the families who come to see Mogel are looking for some serious help. Lots of problems are expressed around eating and meals. When parents complain about their children's eating habits, she asks them about their own. She finds parents who see "bad" foods as evil, and parents who obsessively monitor their children's food intake all day then pig out themselves after the kids have gone to bed. She shares what she's learned as a parent herself. Making time for family, time for meals, keeping a sense of what is transitory and what is really important, maintaining links with her spiritual and ethnic background; these things have helped in her own life.

She brings it back to a Jewish perspective. "By preparing special foods and setting the table with special care for Shabbat dinner, the mystics say that we get a taste of the world to come." Then she tells me about her ninety-year-old aunt. "Her granddaughter is putting together a book that she'll give her, about everybody's memories of her. I was surprised at how I remembered the food that she made, even though she was said to be a bad cook. The food that she made, to the eight-year-old me, seemed wonderful."

Mogel writes that, since the destruction of the ancient Temple in Jerusalem, the place of greatest holiness has become not the synagogue but our own homes. "One traditional Jewish expression for home is the same as the word for a house of worship: *mikdash me'at*, or 'little holy place.' Our dining table with our children is an altar. It has the potential to be the holiest spot on the planet."

Thinking of our plain old table, whether it's made of Formica or wood or even marble, as that little holy place, doesn't mean that we, or our children, are angels. Quite the contrary. It means that, as we enjoy our food and our families, as we sometimes bicker or zone out, we have some place, some thing, some people to come back to. By being fully, joyfully human, we can infuse the divine with the daily, the daily with the divine.

— 7 —

Through All the Years

WHEN MY KIDS were small, we bought a chair that was so ingenious, we stretched our nonexistent furniture budget to include it. Built of sturdy wood, you could remove and add various pieces in different configurations to accommodate anyone from an infant to a smallish adult.

Supper is like that, minus the expense and the Allen wrench. Here are a few examples of how the occasion, like that magic chair, can shift shape to support the changing you.

D-I-V-O-R-C-E

When I ask my friend Lili an open-ended question about supper, she volunteers that one of the most wonderful memories of her childhood was coming home to have supper waiting. Walking into the house and smelling roast chicken; it didn't get much better than that.

Now Lili is a single mom with a high-stress job and two teenagers. When she comes home from work, her daughter always sits and eats with her. Her son, on the other hand, sits with her for a few minutes, then takes his plate of food and goes into his room.

I ask her, How does he do it; where does he eat? I am trying to imagine eating supper in the bedroom, a scenario I hear about a lot, but cannot picture. Where does he put the food, I wonder. On the desk? The night table? The bed?

But then Lili explains that she doesn't really mean *his* room, she means the family room. "He watches TV; he does his homework. He calls it his office."

Now I see. Lili is long divorced from the children's father. Although they see their dad, the concept of a live-in adult male is long gone. And so, it seems, is supper. It looks like Lili's son is creating his own space, in some way being "the man." Lili says that, before the divorce, the family all ate supper together. The meal sort of fell apart in its aftermath.

Because I know that Lili is a wise and devoted mother, I ask her, since supper is no longer a common activity, if she has some other time when she regularly talks to her son. "Oh yes," she offers. "I go in and talk to him afterward."

So Lili's family has worked out its own scenario: a few minutes of togetherness, a nice long mother–daughter chat, a son making an effort to distance himself; a mother who lets him go, but only so far.

Divorce often spells the end not only of the nuclear family, but also of the family meal. There's that startlingly empty chair. There's that sadness that, no matter how bad things were in the marriage, no matter how much life might be improved, a family has, in fact, ruptured. My sense is that, quite often, the supper table is one of those flash points where the new reality can't be ignored, where the regret rises and hangs above the surface, like smog. So it feels easier to let the whole thing drop.

If you live in a family postdivorce, this may be the time to get creative. You can acknowledge the sadness but put some effort into reconfiguring your new family life. Buy a round table.

Move the furniture. Give your kids more responsibility for food decisions, food preparation. As I have said before, rituals both make and mark transitions — not only the small ones, from day to evening, but also the big ones, as families change. Have the new family make a list of their favorite dinner foods, then work at including them all. Try the appreciation technique: Ask each person around the table to say what she appreciates that day. It might be phrased in the negative (*I appreciate that no one is...*), but it can be a good format for moving ahead, keeping things positive. And remember that, in times of stress and change, habits offer real comfort. If we are feeling awkward and uncertain, we at least have some "givens" to count on.

And nothing is as comforting as food. Maybe it's time for Lili to produce some roast chicken, whether she has cooked it herself or bought it at the supermarket and warmed it up. The point is the wonderful aroma, which signifies welcome and home.

BLENDED FAMILIES: STIR, SHAKE, SIMMER, CHILL, GEL

When Marion Lindblad-Goldberg was in her thirties, she married a widower with three elementary-school-age children. Although she had no children of her own, and had never been married, she did have a head start: a career as a family therapist. She now directs the Philadelphia Child and Family Therapy Training Center. Years ago, when she joined her new ready-made family, one of the first things she did was to ask where the children's mother had sat at the dinner table.

"I was not going to take her place," she says. "I had another chair put at the table between two kids who fought anyway. One of the cardinal rules of stepfamilies is, you never displace the biological parent."

Which is a great rule. However, a stepparent will still find herself doing many of the things that the parent used to do (or is still doing, on a different night of the week). The first time one of her new children had a birthday, Lindblad-Goldberg was very careful to find out what kind of cake the child liked. She thought she was doing an exemplary job when she emerged with the cake and the candles, singing Happy Birthday, until the kids started yelling, "No, Mar! You sing after you cut the cake!"

Lindblad-Goldberg learned as she went. She says she is not a great cook, but luckily the children's mother hadn't been, either. "She was a professional like me. So it wasn't Mom's meatballs; it was Ruby's." (Ruby was their housekeeper.)

Still, there were cultural issues. The family she moved into is Jewish; she is not. But again, she did her homework. "I had the girls' maternal grandmother teach me how to make a kugel [pudding]. My sister-in-law taught me how to make challah [ceremonial bread]. I proudly made it for the first seder." Unfortunately, the Passover seder commemorates the Jews' hasty flight from Egypt, with no time for the bread to rise. The whole point of the holiday is to *not* eat bread; it is strictly forbidden.

You might say a stepparent can't win. You might also add that thinking in terms of winning or losing is not a good plan. Keeping a grip on your expectations will probably help you more in the long run.

Lindblad-Goldberg-the-professional says, "If the kid's really unhappy about the divorce, it really doesn't matter what you do. There's no magic solution." In her therapeutic work, she sees these scenarios play out over decades, with, for example, a now-middle-age daughter causing a family rift over the proper recipe for stuffing.

We can say, rather smugly, that it isn't really about stuffing; it's about loyalty, trust, love — whatever stuffing represents in that particular family. Still, it doesn't surprise us that a rift opens up around something to eat. No symbol is more powerful than food. Family battles — encoded as they may be — often play out around the supper table. When families face each other, and the occasion is eating, if things are going poorly, there is no escape.

Evan Imber-Black, a family therapist and coauthor of a book about rituals, says, "When kids are talking about the cooking, they're making a different statement. They can't say the words, *I miss my mother, I wish things were different.*" So they complain about the food.

Lindblad-Goldberg recommends trying to understand how the child feels — although, she acknowledges, "It's very hard for people just trying to be decent stepparents and feeling very unappreciated." She stresses flexibility, talking to the kids, and not forcing them to conform to the stepparent's ideal. "If one parent does the fast food, and the other is a real nutrition nut, and the nutrition nut has the kids three days a week, maybe one of those days, have pizza. It's the relation-ship that's more important than the nutrition. Kids survive. It just takes time. You shouldn't personalize it."

In a remarriage with two sets of children, Lindblad-Goldberg suggests getting them together and saying, "Let's create a menu list. Let's come up with some decisions about meals." You could serve the foods that the kids from family A like on one night, the foods that the kids from family B like the next. By doing that, you're letting the kids know that, although you are establishing rules and expectations, they will be heard. You might even be able to create a Menu C — foods that both sets of kids enjoy.

Here is where supper can be really helpful, sneaking up and allowing you act things out. Imber-Black writes, "Ritual works as both a maintainer and creator of social structure . . . [it] combines doing with believing." Let me repeat that: It combines doing with believing. If you expect the family to do this thing together regularly, they will begin to see themselves as a group that does this thing together regularly.

Sitting down together and sharing a meal is both symbolic and real. It creates an image — us around the supper table — which is rooted in messy reality — us around the supper table. Stepparents in particular must balance those two aspects: the image and the much-less-than-perfect reality. Lindblad-Goldberg talks about a stepparent knocking herself out to make an incredible meal, which the kids fail to duly appreciate, which then leaves the parent feeling resentful and less likely to put together the simple meal that the kids are more likely to want, if in fact they want anything realistic from the stepparent at all. "Most kids like the spaghetti their mothers made. You could make the most exquisite thing in the world. It doesn't matter. It may not taste the same."

For Lindblad-Goldberg, a generation has passed. Now, decades into a good relationship with her stepchildren, she can admit, "I can't say that I never fell into the trap of trying to please through food." She talks about a recent trip a daughter and grandchildren made to visit Lindblad-Goldberg and her husband on vacation in rural Nova Scotia. The visit was to last for only four days, but she had large expectations: "I wanted so much for them to have the experience of a grandmother who is very tuned in to their needs." She wanted to introduce them to the wonderful local fish and lobster. But, because the grandchildren are strictly macaroni-and-cheese types, she wanted them to feel comfortable. So, in preparation, she bought it all. She bought everything. The store had never rung up such a large sale. "We literally broke the cash register," she says. Luckily, she laughs as she tells me the tale.

TEENAGERS!

I call up the high school in my town with the idea of talking informally to a bunch of kids. I've heard so much from strung-out or outraged adults about the impossibility of supper, as well as about the critical importance of supper, that I want to hear what the meal situation sounds like from the kids' point of view.

The principal says that, if I come to his office a few days hence, he will bring me over to study hall and introduce me around. Fine. Except that, when I show up, he is not there. He is hours late, returning from a meeting halfway across the state.

When he does rush in, apologetic, trailing kids and teachers all eager for his time, he runs me over to the cafeteria which, after lunch, is used for study hall. "I'm interested that you're writing about that," he says, as we fast-walk down the corridor. "Why? Do you think that people don't do it? Is it over?" He nods, keeps moving. "Not just the meal, the communication."

By the time we get to the cafeteria it is empty; it is being prepared for an evening event. There are no kids there, and the principal has his whole morning's work to catch up on. Back in the main office, he grabs a kid who's walked in. "This is what you want," he says, introducing him to me.

This is not what I asked for, a single kid who, judging by the smiles on everyone's faces, is one of the good ones. Not that I'm looking for problem kids, just a cross section. And there is the added small-town conundrum — when he mentions the kid's last name, it clicks. I know his mother. Not well, just enough to know how hard she's tried to be a good mom. But I give the kid, whom I'll call K, what I hope is a warm professional smile, and don't let on that his name rings a bell. I tell him anonymity is fine; I just want to get a sense of what supper is like for his family, and for the families of his friends.

K, who is a senior, is an athlete, good looking and friendly, the next-to-youngest of four. He tells me that he's unusual in that his parents are divorced, and he splits his week between two houses. On the days he spends at his dad's house, when he comes home from sports practice, his father has supper ready. His dad tries to wait, so everyone can eat together. On Sundays, he says, his mom goes all-out. They have a big dinner. And no, they never have the TV on, except sometimes when the Patriots are playing.

When his parents first divorced, quite some time ago, his mom would get home from work "really tired, really stressed out. She'd make something, beef and broccoli, but if we didn't want it we would eat something else; cereal or ramen noodles." I ask what they did about his father's seat. It got taken by K's older brother.

Little by little, his mother's life became more organized.

"She wasn't as stressed out coming home. She was more open to what we wanted for dinner." Now, although not everybody likes everything served, they eat from what's on the table. There's been another change as well — the Dad chair is occupied by Mom's live-in boyfriend. "It was weird at first," K says.

I've met this man, only briefly. He and the mom seem to care for each other a lot.

I ask what things were like at K's father's house after the divorce.

"At my dad's house, he never cooked. We ate like freezer food or take-out. I think that's what a lot of dads are like after a divorce." Now I ask him how many of his friends' parents are divorced, and he tells me almost all. Interesting that at first he was apologetic about it, when it's so pervasive.

He says by this time, his dad has developed his cooking skills. "Now he cooks every night. I'm actually a cook," he adds. "I think that stems from my mom always needing help from that period of time. We all learned." An older sibling, no longer living at home, now calls their mom for recipes.

I ask if most of his friends eat supper with their families or just move through the kitchen. It's definitely the latter, he says, and adds that he feels like they're missing something. "You're not offered that family connection I'm offered."

When I ask if anything replaces it, I'm thinking about whether the families who don't share a meal get together in some other way. But he is thinking more concretely — what do kids eat — and says that the teenagers eat with their friends. Most often they drive to Jim's Roast Beef. (Meat. White bread. Fries. Soda.) So no, it's not like there's a conscious choice in the family: *We can't do dinner, so we'll do . . . x.* I know that, for lots of parents, by the time their kids are teenagers, they run out of steam. Pick your battles, they advise each other wearily.

Then K continues, "I enjoy having dinner with my parents because [of] the love that they've shown me . . . ," and I am blown away. I had been asking him about nuts and bolts, and he has cut to the heart of things. "I know the amount of time my mom's put into me; it makes me feel good. I like to sit down with her. I think the more respect a parent shows to their child, the more apt they are to sit down and talk and have dinner with them. I know if my dad or mom's not treating me right, I'm not gonna want to sit down with them."

Again, as to why some kids don't eat with their families, K offers: "Some kids are just big socializers. They can't find the time to sit down with their families. Instead of having an argument, they [the parents] just let it slide by." I want to call up each of those parents personally. Don't they know how much their kids still need to talk to them? Don't they realize how hard it is to find a vegetable at Jim's?

I ask if sometimes his friends come home with him for supper. Yes, he says. Although, when they do, the conversation changes. "If my mom hasn't seen him [the friend] in a while, she asks how he is, what's he been doing." Normal conversation, by contrast, is "things that occurred in our day, what we did." I get a sense that, when a friend is over, he misses that daily catching up. Then he continues, "There's a little time in your day, in your lives, your whole family's together and doing one thing. It's a time to like share with everyone. I can talk with my brothers all at once and hear all their input." I am wishing I hadn't taken the anonymity tack. I am wishing I could call up K's mom and tell her what a great job she's done.

I wonder about the mechanics of their suppers: Who does what jobs; is there a way their family starts or ends the meal? In his family, the jobs are stable, and yes, the kids always fight about them. The youngest one gets the easiest task.

"My mom's always the last one to sit down, to have her food on her plate. We wait for her to start eating. We ask if can we be excused." I ask how his mom enforces those rules. "I don't even remember when that started. I was so young. I just picked up on it."

I tell him that obviously supper is very important to him, largely because of the talking, and yet it seems like the things they talk about aren't earth shattering. The family isn't exchanging secrets, or expressing their innermost thoughts; they're just talking about their day. K agrees, but can't explain it any more. It's something he counts on, he says.

So it's that very dailiness, that ordinariness, that make it important, making it a given in K's life. Seeing his parents, seeing his siblings, getting everyone's attention, having everyone check in. It's solid. It's there.

Thank goodness the high school principal was wrong. In my town, communication isn't all gone. One family, at least, is doing quite well.

COMINGS AND GOINGS

I am getting anxious e-mails from my friend Jon, who is facing what he calls The Last Family Supper. Although his son isn't leaving for college for months, he says that he and his wife have begun to think about every supper that way. Although teenagers about to leave home can provide their own brand of misery, families who have weathered the storms of adolescence without getting shipwrecked now find themselves looking at each other across the table and thinking about The End.

I want to tell Jon and Deb that they are both right and wrong to be sad and concerned. They are correct in thinking that, once their son leaves, their little nuclear family will never be the same again. But that does not mean that the next stage of life won't be good. I would bet anything their son will be showing up on occasion, sometimes with new friends in tow. In time, they will even be able to visit him. Day-to-day, though, the family center will definitely shift. The child still at home will get more attention, which he may or may not appreciate. ("No, really, didn't anything interesting happen today?") Whoever is responsible for the grocery shopping will get a reprieve. And, if things seem a bit dull, they may also feel more roomy, civil, and subdued. Also, after years of self-denial, parents can occasionally do things just because they want to.

Another friend had a different response to her firstborn heading off to college — she pretty much gave up cooking. Although Judy had always been a good cook, she had just had enough. Even though she still had a high schooler at home, she took this opportunity to abdicate her role as, in my father's old-fashioned phrase, chief cook and bottle washer. She figured that, in a house with two adults and one remaining teen, everyone could just manage for themselves.

Supper became haphazard, a victim of shifting schedules and primary-cook burnout. And then a surprising thing happened: Judy's husband stepped in and filled the void. David didn't like the aimless wandering through the kitchen. He decided to give cooking a try, and it didn't take him long to figure out that he liked it. He says that, although he hadn't ever cooked before, he had spent enough years watching first his mother, and then his wife, perform their everyday magic around the stove.

Now, a decade later, David has taken over all the cooking, and has turned into an ambitious chef. With just his wife and himself at home, mealtime can be more flexible; he can put some time into a special dish. His most recent birthday present from his eldest child was an Indian cookbook, along with some of the more exotic ingredients he would need to produce the East Asian dishes. His wife is relieved. Life after children comes with lots of surprises.

In my own case, the big change came when our younger child went off to college. That first fall, my husband could not bear to eat supper at home; he wanted to go out to a restaurant every single night. I found his unhappiness touching, even as I fretted over our credit card bills.

I had the opposite reaction: I was damned well going to keep my homemaking turf even in the face of a diminishing home. I reminded myself of a woman I had once interviewed for a cooking feature when I was a newspaper reporter. A great local cook, she was in her sixties, divorced, and living alone. In her mind, however, she was still married and raising four children. She told me she couldn't break herself of the habit of cooking for a mob. She showed me her fridge. Like an alcoholic who knows she should be going to AA, she had it stuffed to the breaking point with leftovers.

In time, my husband and I settled into a new routine — later dinnertime, a shift in menu, lots of dinners out; sometimes just the two of us, sometimes with friends. The fact that we can do things at the last minute still makes me giddy. At breakfast and lunch, when we happen to be home, we are likely to sit in any old seat, but at supper we still take the Mom and Dad places. It just feels good.

LINEN NAPKIN FOR ONE

Joan Wickersham, who is in her sixties and has been widowed for years, lives alone, but her days are quite busy. She is president of the National Society of Colonial Dames of America, an organization that restores and preserves historic properties, and sponsors research and educational programs. "We have sixteen thousand members," she says. "They don't all call me, but I do get a lot of calls."

At seven every evening, she leaves her home office, walks downstairs, and gets her dinner ready. When she sits down to eat in the living room, by herself, she turns the phone off, except for the times she's expecting a call from one of her children. "I don't consider it a solitary supper," she explains. "I call it dining alone." She sets out a tray with a linen napkin, much as she did when she and her husband used to eat together. "I eat alone a lot. I like it. I don't mind my own company, and I like my own cooking. I like messing around in the kitchen." She isn't tempted by prepared foods, which she finds expensive. She is always trying new recipes because, she says, she gets bored.

And she cares how things look. "I feel very strongly about having the china match. If I'm having more than one glass of wine, I'll put it in a carafe." She does have a small TV in the living room, which she watches while she eats her dinner, even though, she says, she has to turn her head to see it. The room is furnished around the fireplace (she makes a fire at dinnertime when the weather is cool), and she doesn't want to feature the TV. When her grandkids are with her, which they are a lot during the summer, they all eat together in the kitchen.

Because Wickersham doesn't like to cook at suppertime, she does her dinner prep either during the day or else after dinner. "I don't just open the refrigerator and just say, *What shall I have tonight*. I was that way as a wife and mother, too. I had dinner all organized before I went out in the morning."

Back then, she says, "I looked forward to the dinner, but it was just another segment of the day." Anyone who has made meals for the family, day in and day out, knows how easy it is for the job part of the meal to overwhelm any sense of occasion.

But now, when I ask Wickersham what would happen if she couldn't have her dinner the way she has come to enjoy it, she says, "I'd be devastated. I really look forward to that quiet wind-down time at the end of the day. I consider it my time, my very own time, and I consider that a luxury." She adds, "Not that I ever minded sharing my time with my beloved husband and my children. When they're here, I don't wish I was eating dinner by myself."

But when we talk about people who buy prepared foods every night, she wonders if they take the food out of the containers when they eat. "It's so sad," she says. "Even if you do it [eat dinner] on the run, it takes quite a lot of time. And why not enjoy it?"

— 8 —

Reports from the Field

WAYZATA, MINNESOTA, population four thousand, is a growing, desirable suburb of Minneapolis on the shores of Lake Minnetonka. The locals pronounce it something like Wee-ZET-ta, shaping their lips in a way that I cannot, for the life of me, master. Like well-endowed suburbs and towns all over, it has lots of moms who stay at home or work part time, lots of divorce, lots of parental involvement in the schools, lots of organized sports. A Friday-night high school football game can easily attract eight thousand fans.

The churches are new and large; the high school, just six years old, is pristine. But most of the time you will find most kids, as well as their chauffering, coaching, cheering parents, on the practice fields, the playing fields, the rinks, the team buses, or in the family cars. An elaborate system of youth leagues that meet after school, on weekends, over school vacations, and throughout the summer feeds into the high school sports network. Traveling teams, which feature hours-long car rides and overnight trips, begin at age seven. Kids are routinely put on hockey skates when they are two, to be ready for teams the next year. And because ice time is at a premium, hockey practice can be scheduled anytime from 6 A.M. to 10 P.M.

These leagues are filled. The prevailing wisdom is that, if your youngster doesn't start a sport the first time it's offered, it is too late. The justification seems to be the value of playing on teams, and the hope of a college athletic scholarship. There is, in addition, a sense that every child must be offered every opportunity, so that any outstanding talent or passion can be discovered and nurtured. It is an article of faith that a child who shows an aptitude for a sport will devote herself to it year-round, with the family schedule adjusted accordingly.

Wayzata is not alone in this fixation. According to the study by the University of Michigan Survey Research Center mentioned before, between 1981 and 1997, children lost twelve hours of free time per week, playtime declined by 25 percent, and time spent in unstructured outdoor activities fell by half. Meanwhile, commitment to structured sports doubled, and time spent watching other people (like siblings) play sports rose fivefold.

In Wayzata, in addition to sports, music is big. There is some theater, and the many churches have active youth programs and choirs. Also heard, when the subject of keeping kids busy comes up: the dangers lurking in the world today, the guilt of working parents, the sheer giddy cornucopia of available options. When there are six different dance schools in town, it's only human nature to assume that your daughter should be signed up with at least one.

I visit Wayzata in early spring, when the lake is beginning to thaw, as the guest of a pioneering organization called Putting Family First (PFF), parents and educators who worry that this lockstep hustle to keep kids busy busy busy has gotten way out of hand. I hear terms like *competitive parenting* and *children as products*. These folks say that, when family life, marriage, and community involvement are defined by children's success, then we are all the poorer for it. It also sends the wrong messages to children: You are the linchpin of our lives. We love you for your achievements. The pie is limited, you'd better grab your share. Don't take time off; don't dawdle, don't daydream. Forget creativity, idiosyncrasy, flashes of genius, doing good deeds, or just plain noodling. If you're not good enough, you won't make the cut.

In this environment, family supper is one more quaint artifact, like vinyl records or manual typewriters. While most parents remember the family meals of their own youth with nostalgic affection, their children are more likely to have pizza in the car, a microwaved, frozen dish eaten in front of the TV in the family room or next to the bedroom computer, or else a sandwich consumed on the sidelines of a sibling's game. Dinner is held hostage to the all-important schedule, with little time or opportunity for talk.

The folks in PFF worry about the loss of family meals, family vacations, family rituals like bedtime. They point to studies like the one in 2000 from the Council of Economic Advisers to the President called *Teens and Their Parents in the 21st Century*: "The largest federally funded study of American teenagers found a strong association between regular family meals (five or more dinners per week with a parent) and academic success, psychological adjustment, and lower rates of alcohol use, drug use, early sexual behavior, and suicidal risk. (Results held for both one parent and two parent families and after controlling for social class factors.)"

The adults who identify with PFF are not the only ones aware of the price paid for all that cheerful activity. When I meet with a group of teenage boys at St. Philip the Deacon

Lutheran Church in Wayzata, they tell me it's common for parents, driving their kids off to college freshman year, to say, "By the way, we're getting divorced." I think, if the kids are joking about this, it must be widespread.

When I had read the Putting Family First Web site from my home in Massachusetts, I conjured an image of a town that had grabbed hold of its rudder and, by sheer force of character, turned things around. But after a few days of meeting with local movers and shakers, I get more of a sense of how brave, how enormous their undertaking has been; how much time it will take to get that rudder to budge. For the past five years, this group has been working with intelligence and doggedness to change Wayzata, but the forces that created this state of affairs have been building for decades, and they come from far beyond Minnesota. Although PFF gets some funding from the state, and from family foundations, for the most part parents just chip in. There is no paid staff, no office. "I think we'd hoped there would be huge changes really fast, but that's part of a grassroots movement," according to Barbara Carlson, president of PFF and my host in Wazyata. She has lived here for three decades, and was raised thirty miles away. She is, to my eyes, iconically midwestern — enthusiastic, resolutely upbeat. She worked as a Sunday school teacher when her kids were little, then took community jobs, both paying and volunteer. If anyone is connected, organized, and focused, it is Carlson. But of her quest for balance, for helping families reclaim simple pleasures like mealtimes, vacations, and bedtime rituals, she says, "It's going to take a long time."

This year, PFF is featured on the calendar for the Wayzata Public Schools. They will be on every family's refrigerator.

They got a local bank to sponsor the calendar so it could be expanded a bit to feature local organizations. Each baby step takes work.

One of the first people I meet is Alice Woog, principal of Wayzata West Middle School and the mother of two grown children. When I arrive, she is skillfully, and tactfully, leading an alternately weeping and snarling seventh-grade boy into her office for a brief chat. A few minutes later, one crisis down, Woog freely admits that, even with nineteen years of principaling behind her, people don't want to listen to what she has to say. She tells me, "For some people, I think it's easier not to spend time with your family. If you keep real busy, you don't have to address issues." There is also the question of the parents' egos. "I am seeing more and more parents making their children their job. I grew up in an immigrant household. My mother only had a sixth-grade education. I knew that we kids, and my father, were the center of her world. But" — she slows down her words for emphasis — "we were not her job." These days, she says, if she is having a disciplinary conference with a child and the child's parents, it is not unusual for the parents to tell their offspring, in front of the principal, "You don't have to listen to her."

But parents are also under siege. The busyness enterprise seems to be fueled by peer pressure — parents lean on other parents to lean on the coaches, who lean on the kids. Miss a practice and you're benched. Miss a game and you're cut. Carlson tells me she regularly hears from parents like the mom who called her recently for advice. The woman was distraught because her mother-in-law had died and she wanted her daughter to attend the funeral. The problem? The funeral would conflict with a softball game — not even a championship. The coach threatened to cut the girl if she missed the game, and then the other team parents called the mother and badgered her to let the girl play. The mother caved, and sent her daughter to play. I am dumbstruck when Carlson tells me this tale, shocked at this mother's lack of confidence and common sense. Carlson, who has been fighting the good fight in a public, organized way for years now, is saddened but not shocked.

In 1998, she tells me, she was running a community parenting forum and invited Bill Doherty to speak. Doherty, a family therapist and professor at the University of Minnesota, had recently written a book, *The Intentional Family*. It contended that "the natural drift of family life in contemporary America is toward slowly diminishing connection, meaning, and community." He said it was "the best and worst of times for families." The worst because "community and culture are unable to provide a coherent vision or set of tools and supports," but the best because "we understand better what makes families work," and we have "unprecedented freedom to shape the kind of family life we want, to be intentional about our families." He urged parents to create and maintain family rituals because they give us "predictability, connection, identity, and a way to enact values." Supper is the family ritual he cites most often.

When Doherty spoke in Wayzata, the parents got so much out of his presentation that, the next year, when it was time to get another speaker, everyone wanted to have him back.

At the same time, Doherty had been looking for a community that was ready to address the issue of overscheduled kids and underconnected families. When I speak to him, he ticks off for me the reasons he decided to work with Wayzata: "It's small enough. It's containable enough. People know each other. When we recruited people, we had the leaders. It's not just a bedroom community that has sprung up in the last fifteen years."

Carlson remembers, "We formed a task force. We had a town meeting with the leaders of the community, the mayor, the police chief, sports and rec, the schools — about eighty-five people." They enlisted the aid of already existing groups like the PTA. They identified who, in the community, would be their champions.

They also reached out to ordinary families. Sue Kakuk remembers feeling relieved to find other like-minded parents. "As a family, it seemed like we had to slow down. The family meals, the vacations; it was kind of frustrating. None of my kids' friends had any restrictions." She had been surprised to learn that her neighbors — a nice middle-class family — not only didn't have suppers, but (classic story) they didn't even have a dining room or kitchen table. Many other families didn't have bedtimes. She and her husband knew what kind of atmosphere they wanted to create for their own kids, but they hadn't found much backup. She says, "When I heard Bill, I said, We're not really alone."

Jane Guffy, whose children were on the young end of the spectrum, wanted to have some advance warning about their futures. But she was already getting a preview: "My kids would be playing at somebody's house and it was dinnertime. I expected them to come home. They would say, 'What do you mean, come home? We're having Pop-Tarts.'" She knew that she could set the standards for her own family but still, she says, "Knowing there was a group of people supporting all of this gave us the backbone to say, Yes, we can do this."

Carol Bergenstal recalls drafting a mission statement. "We wanted to make sure people didn't think we were a religious group per se, or were anti-sports. The family structure is the essence of democracy. If families don't take time to share values and beliefs, those tenets of our being get lost." And Carlson remembers, from the beginning, "trying to be mindful that there are different forms of families." They wanted to empower parents, not give them one rigid model or yet another set of standards they couldn't meet.

The early projects of Putting Family First were extremely ambitious. They offered a Seal of Approval to an organization that fostered family life. They published a Family Consumer Guide to Kids' Activities that rated more than a hundred classes and teams on the basis of the time, money, and travel required. It also listed which activities made it easy for families to maintain their dinnertime. Still, their introduction said, "We recognize that each family must make decisions about what works best. We will not tell families what to do nor will we blame parents who want to enrich their children's lives with activities."

Almost as soon as the organization got off the ground, it received a lot of national attention — coverage by the *New York Times* and most of the national women's magazines. Doherty and Carlson coauthored a book, *Putting Family First*. Now, after four years of working with Wayzata, Doherty has moved on to coach two other Minnesota communities.

PFF is still a loosely knit volunteer organization without formal membership, operating out of a post office box and a Web site. When they need money to fund an activity or event, the leaders simply chip in. They laugh when they get requests from around the country to come in and set up PFF branches. Two things they have learned in their time together: (1) Schedule board meetings at lunchtimes, so as not to take away even more family time. (2) No one is going to fight this fight for you.

Although Carlson says, "For a while, we wondered were we really making a difference," to an outsider it is obvious that they have created a strong public presence. They keep the issues front and center. They have become a critical mass, the virtual address for anyone in town concerned with these problems. It makes a huge difference to families like the Johnsons.

Anne Johnson planned to serve me a family supper at home but, because my visit falls on Ash Wednesday, she has had to schedule me around an evening church service that follows the weekly meeting of her son's church youth group.

Wednesday has traditionally been Church Night in Wayzata, the time when youth groups and choruses meet. In the past, schools didn't give homework on Wednesday nights, but this practice has died out. The Johnsons' church, Wayzata Community Church, normally serves a family supper to a couple of hundred families every Wednesday at big tables in the church basement, to make the evening run a little more smoothly.

But on Ash Wednesday, there is no supper served. So I join the Johnsons in the empty church basement as they spend a tightly scheduled fifteen minutes together eating the supper — sandwiches, slices of fruit, carrots and celery, individual bottles of water — that Anne has brought from home. She has also brought, for me to see, a spiral-bound book, *Keep Talking*, written by a pair of Minnesota women, that offers conversational topics for families who are running dry.

My heart goes out to Anne and her husband, Jeff, who are trying so hard. And their children are real, normal kids, not poster children for family togetherness. Six-year-old Lia has a hard time not squirming. Nine-year-old Reilly seems droopy after a long day, while I can almost hear eleven-year-old Max counting the number of seconds he has to stay in his seat before running off with his friends. Still, when their parents prompt them, all three kids answer a stranger's questions politely, and Max tries to say something genuinely kind about his sister.

The Johnsons try to have supper together every night, although recently Jeff's job has required a lot of traveling. When he's not there, Anne and the kids eat together.

Their moment of truth came last summer. The summer before that one had been grim for Anne: "Three different kids at three different sports at three different places." And that was in the evenings, after days spent at camp or in class. "The kids knew how unhappy I was," Anne says, "driving them around all the time." A voluble woman with dark, curly hair, Anne had a career as a pharmaceutical sales rep before staying home to raise her children.

This past year, they made a tough decision: no organized evening activities for the kids during the summer.

"The kids don't give us a hard time," Anne says. But the couple's friends do. Still, Anne remembers this past summer fondly. "Evenings were just for the family," she says. "We'd do the bike rides, the beaches." However, they were the only family they knew who did that. "Most of the kids are booked from morning till night. When we don't schedule our kids and say, Just find somebody in the neighborhood to play with, there is just nobody in the neighborhood."

Anne, who was one of seven children, grew up in rural Minnesota. When she was in school, all the extracurricular activities were school based, so she could take the "activities bus" and be home by five. After supper, everyone stayed home. But this generation has done an about-face. Her sister in Atlanta has two girls. "They made the decision their girls are going to be soccer players," so the family spends all its free time at practices and games. "That's family togetherness for them," Anne says. One of her brothers has three boys. "They live and die their sports. I don't think they ever have a family meal. My brother in Tucson, they tried to have one Sunday supper a month together. It didn't work."

What makes the Johnsons different, I ask. Is it confidence? Jeff smiles. "Or laziness, or stupidity. Or confidence that in the long run . . . what we're trying to do is more beneficial than going the other way. I don't think we have world-class athletes [in our children]. I think there are a lot of kids that are out there are going to be extremely disappointed and have nothing to fall back on other than what they've been training for all their life."

Anne admits, "It's terribly gut wrenching to make these decisions. We may be completely wrong."

But Jeff adds, "Even if we are completely wrong, there's not that much to lose. So they can't shoot a jump shot, but they can roll up a sleeping bag. Big deal. It doesn't really seem like our kids are differently developed than other kids."

Anne says, "It feels right to us, and feels good with the kids, and that's why we do it."

But it is obvious that their effort is taking a lot of strength. When I ask them if, apart from the Putting Family First people, they are alone in this, they answer, wearily, "Yes."

I am in no position to judge. On my visit to Wayzata, I only meet the family-friendly people. In Bugs Peterschmidt's sunny kitchen, with its flowered wallpaper and its pig motif, she tells me how it took her coming down with walking pneumonia a few years back to get her family to slow down. That year, she was relieved to find that, when the sign-up sheet came for soccer, her son said, "I don't want to do it. I don't want to do anything where I have to get into a car."

Now they have a maximum of two activities per kid. And at supper, at their kitchen table, they light candles to give a sense of formality, of wonder, of time-out-of-time. Fifteen-year-old Max, who lights the candles, has been given the title of fire facilitator, while twelve-year-old Betsy is the aesthetic forewoman. (She sets the table.) They have a dinner pig, a small stone in a porcine shape. The pig gets passed to whoever has the worst manners that night. When Peterschmidt looks for the little creature to show it to me, she can't find it. With a laugh, she tells me that Max has probably hidden it again.

Since the Peterschmidts limited their kids' extracurricular commitments, they have found more time for their extended family. They established a new, updated version of Sunday dinner, a custom that had died out. Now four families take turns hosting a monthly meal of what Peterschmidt calls comfort food. And the comfort does not just come on the plates. Now that Sunday dinners have started up again, her mother figures she's been cooking them for sixty-eight years. This brings up the subject of Great-Aunt Lila, who lived to be a hundred. Peterschmidt passes along Lila's secrets: She ate lard every day, and she never carried a grudge.

As I leave, I notice the Peterschmidts' dining room table,

covered with a series of black-and-white photos of behind-the-scenes preparations for a family wedding that took place sixty years ago. Her husband recently found them, and is reprinting the good ones, so he can hand them out at the next Sunday dinner.

Next I meet with a Lutheran pastor, John Hogenson, a tall, trim, dark-haired man who has come to this post in Wayzata from a succession of small-town parishes. He says things are no less pressured there. Because the rural population is smaller, everyone has to do everything. And when kids travel for games, they must trek even greater distances. There is one difference, though. In Wayzata, he says, "The image I have is almost like emotionally hyperventilating, almost catching their breath. I see parents here much more intentional, but they're kind of going warp speed. They have a sense they have to do it perfectly."

Hogenson and his wife have chosen a different tack: "When we moved here, we decided to slow everything down." Still, because of his three daughters, he says, "I'm learning a lot about dance and skating." But family suppers remain central. He has learned that, instead of asking the generic What did you do today, he should be a bit more specific: Anybody get in trouble today? Anything funny happen? Another ploy is to ask about one of his daughters' friends: What did so-and-so do today? "Otherwise," he explains, "you get pretty short answers."

The Hogensons try to keep their meals healthy, but are subject to the same pressures as everyone else. Because I meet the Reverend Hogenson on Ash Wednesday, a working day for ministers, he explains that he will have only a short supper break before he has to get back to the church. And because his wife is on the sofa with back pain, Hogenson tells me ruefully, "I think it's Pizza Hut tonight."

In sports-minded Wayzata, Putting Family First has found some of its most important allies on the football field. Both Brad Anderson, the football coach at Wayzata High School, and David Gaither, area director of the local youth league, are strong-minded, principled leaders who have a deep understanding of the real value of sports. Although I meet them individually, I see how powerful the synergy of like-minded people can be.

Anderson is a friendly, earnest man wearing a neat striped shirt and chinos who coaches track and football, and teaches biology and genetics as well. But football is the glamour sport in this part of the world, and that is where Anderson shines. He graduated from Wayzata himself, and makes sure to tell me about his debt to *his* coach, who first showed him that strong values and clear priorities could create an atmosphere for winning football. Because, while supper and family time are all very nice, fans here want successful teams.

"There's strong pressure in this community to be not only competitive but excellent," Anderson says. Luckily, Wayzata is usually in the top five to ten teams in the state. "We have one graduate now playing for the Denver Broncos. Next year we'll have eight Division One football players playing. A lot will play Division Two, which is still a scholarship-type program."

He tells me that, at the beginning of every season, he gives his students, and their parents, a copy of the year's practice and game schedule, along with his expectations of how he, the students, and the parents, should behave. And he is up front about his priorities. "At the top is the faith obligation. That is always honored first. If you had to miss football for going to a retreat, no question. Second is family." He says that, if a student misses a practice or game for a family wedding or reunion, there will be no repercussions. "The third priority is schoolwork. The fourth is football." He says he always tries to have his players finished with their practice by five o'clock, a controversial move in a region where other school districts keep their players until seven-thirty every night.

As to his clearly delineated priorities, Anderson says, "I kind of feel like when things are in the right order they [the players] have fewer problems. It allows them to be more focused on football when they are playing. When we get them we get all their attention, not just part of their attention." But he admits that it's not all smooth sailing. He objects when parents pull kids out of practice for trivial matters, when he has built a system on trust.

Carlson, who has taken me to meet Anderson, wants to know if it's necessary for kids to start at age five. Absolutely not, he tells us, citing burnout and injuries. He sees no advantage to playing one sport year-round. He tells us about his two daughters, nine and eleven, whom he limits to "one activity at a time, one of some type of arts, whether it's choir or taking piano lessons." He also thinks it's a mistake for so many parents to push their children toward college athletic scholarships. "You hear a lot of stories about kids being destroyed in the process." He makes another important point. "We live in a community where we have a number of ex-professional-athletes." These are not the parents pushing for more-more-more.

Next we turn to the topic of spring break, a time when, after a long, cold winter, many Minnesota families eagerly look forward to getting away. But many sports hold practices over vacations, and demote or drop youngsters who opt for the family trip. Anderson, the track coach, holds the line. He does not discipline kids who take family vacations.

Still, he always feels the pressure to begin practices earlier and earlier in the season. He calls it "an arms race. If softball does it, soccer has to answer back. Then communities are racing against each other. . . . As a parent, you're put into a vise. By yourself, you really have no clout to change things." But now, he says, with Putting Family First, "we have a chance for a little sanity. We use it in our youth program as a selling point, [that] we follow these guidelines."

But Anderson has no illusions. "I think, in this community, if we didn't win, I wouldn't be here long."

David Gaither is a busy man. He's just been elected to the state legislature. He has a business that conducts executive searches and helps in something called organizational pathology. He's the area coordinator and chairman of the board for the Wayzata Plymouth Youth Football Association, which has more than 150 coaches and seven hundred kids in grades four through eight. He is trim and fit, an ex-athlete who looks the part.

Still, when he meets with Carlson and me for breakfast, before he talks about football, he wants to say something about supper.

"When I was a kid, when we ate supper at my grandparents, we'd sit around afterward playing a game called I Remember When. My grandma would say, 'I remember when the ice man would come to the house and deliver ice.' My mom would say, 'I remember when there was food rationing.'"

Gaither tells us that, when he was younger, he really enjoyed listening to how things had changed. It helped him understand something of history in very personal terms. Even now he smiles as he remembers the relaxed comfort of those sitting-around times.

He also recalls neighborhood baseball games, when a team could have any number of players, depending on how many kids were around. One boy in the neighborhood had cerebral palsy; the rules were altered when it was his turn to play. And he remembers those times not only with nostalgia, but also with the analytical mind of someone trained to see the big picture. The decisions that kids made about team size, about suspension of rules, were critical in their maturing.

"Quite frankly, we're managing out leadership," he says. His argument is that, if adults are always in charge, kids don't learn management skills like organizing, taking initiative, accepting responsibility. Parental involvement can be a good, he says, but he faults parents who try to influence coaches, or who push for more and more practices. "Let's not make this a vocation," he says. "Let's make this an extra that's enjoyable."

As much as managing kids, Gaither says that his job is managing parents, which his organization does by limiting practice times and compressing the season. They make sure kids get equal playing time and are distributed evenly on all teams. Like Anderson at the high school, he spells out his priorities to kids and parents: "Your faith, your family, your school, your football."

Gaither's league has encouraged cooperation on and off the field. They needed someplace to store equipment, so to raise money for a building they stopped handing out trophies and started selling T-shirts. They were able to build a building that they now share with the high school. And several different youth sports are actually joining together to raise money to light the playing fields. This will allow more flexibility in scheduling practices, so more families will be able to have supper together.

One more thing: Gaither has no illusions about the athletic scholarship route. He had a Division One scholarship for football and track, the only such student in a class of five hundred. But, he says, "If you, as a parent, are hoping you'll get this, you are far better served by piano lessons.

"In basketball, 1 percent of the kids playing high school basketball will have a Division One position. One percent of Division One players go on to the NBA. The average playing time in the NBA is three years. You're better off putting the money in the casino."

His son is a high school sophomore who wants to play quarterback. "I tell him, Let's go on a career path. He's number one in his math class, gets straight A's. I tell him, Your probability of succeeding here [as a quarterback] are low. Your probability of succeeding there [as a math student] are high."

I hope it is Gaither's balanced approach that accounts for his league's success. He says that his numbers have been growing every year, even though school numbers are stable. Most important, he says, "My mom factor is high." In other words, parents appreciate his efforts.

As to his support for Putting Family First, he calls it, "missionary work. Things matter to me. My dad said, Leave things better than you found them."

Now that he's in the state legislature, he wants to improve sports opportunities for kids all over the state. And he wants to keep the values up front. "It's a far better thing to teach kids how to play the game than to win the championship."

My last night in Wayzata, Sue Kakuk, who runs the PFF Web site, treats me to a wonderful supper at her house prepared by her teenage daughter, Alynn. (In the Kakuk house, Thursday is Mom's night off.) The entrée, a creamy chicken and pasta dish, is a new one for the Kakuks, who love to try different recipes. They've been tracking every Thursday-night supper for several years. The most memorable invention may have been PEZ soup, concocted a couple of years back by Kakuk's son, Karl, now twelve. Various combinations of Kakuks enter, and win, cooking contests. They have won a trip to California, a set of bunk beds, and, in a jackpot from Paul Newman, new playground equipment for their school.

The supper is yummy: the pasta, the salad, the banana cream pie that, I hear, got made in a rush late last night, with some help from Mom. I love the way that, on Thursday nights, the Kakuks use the antique glassware they inherited. I enjoy how they sit around after supper, long enough for a guest to learn about Karl's obsession with duct tape, and to see the backpack he uses every day, which is made out of nothing but the folded silvery material. Jay, the dad, is an engineer, so there may be a tinkering gene at work. After the family leaves the table, they sit together for a bit in the living room and read aloud from books that help them dream about, and plan, their summer vacation.

As I leave the Kakuks' home in the dark night, my sense is that many families in Wayzata are still rushing around in their cars. But at least those, like the Kakuks, who would rather spend some time together no longer have to apologize for what they are doing. Is this world crazy, or what?

RIDGEWOOD, NEW JERSEY: READY, SET, RELAX

March 26, 2002, may well be a day that will live in irony. After a whole year of planning, suburban Ridgewood, New Jersey, celebrated its first Family Night. Families were urged to relax and spend time together — no agenda, no schedule, no checklist, no prize. Extracurricular activities — sports, tutoring, religious education, music lessons — all were canceled, homework assignments in elementary and middle schools shelved, so that families could, for one short period, spend time with each other doing whatever they wanted to do.

This simple plan came from a local mom and was promoted as a home-grown happening. But once word got out, the event struck a chord with harried parents around the country. Most people noted that it took a full year of planning for this town of twenty-five thousand to organize a night off. Some local folks were offended that they were being told what to do, even though the organizers made it very clear that they had no specific plan or goal. Even those who appreciated the break put it in context. One "grateful parent" wrote to the organizing committee, "The whole country is talking about our Ridgewood Family Night! Should we be happy about that? Or should we be a bit embarrassed that we needed encouragement?"

It started rather simply. Marcia Marra is a mother of three school-age children who has lived in town for a dozen years. She works part time at a local family counseling agency, as manager of community initiatives. Her job is to think about which problems are personal, which are political, which are both, with a goal of improving the quality of family life. For Marra it was a no-brainer that the biggest obstacle was time — not enough of it. Not for her family, not for the families in her town. "I just felt personally as a worker, this whole running-around thing was putting a lot of stress on family."

As was the case in Wayzata, the visit of an "expert" galvanized public feeling. Alvin Rosenfeld, author of *Hyper-Parenting* (also issued in a paperback edition titled *The Overscheduled Child*), had given a talk at the high school, and Marra put together a committee to discuss the issues he raised. The group, which included the heads of all the PTAs as well as all the local religious leaders, "ended up spending a lot of time talking about how it affects us," Marra recalls. "We really felt it was such a cultural issue, we had to involve the whole community." But because they didn't have any easy fixes, they decided to start small. "We didn't have a lot of solutions to offer."

When they came up with the idea of having one night that families could spend together, Marra says, "We tried not to be judgmental; we wanted to keep it lighthearted." If families went out to eat, that was fine. If they ordered in and watched a movie, that was okay, too. "We wanted to give them a night off, not put pressure on them."

In terms of publicity, their goal was to get coverage from their local paper. But the news of a night without watching the clock traveled far beyond Ridgewood. First, when the event was still in the planning stage, the group got a write-up in the New Jersey section of the *New York Times*. Then, two days before the stay-at-home evening, the Associated Press picked up the story. Marra remembers being flabbergasted by all the attention: "Here I'm like this regular mom. I got a call from someone who said they were from *Good Morning America*. I thought they were joking. But then, when I was talking to them, I got a call on the other line from the *Today* show." National print media was not far behind.

In addition to the breadth of the coverage, Marra was surprised by how seriously local families took the event. Parents who were out of town on business that night worried about whether they could make it up another time. Some who worked in the evening asked if they could do it at breakfast, or over the weekend. A few single parents wondered if there was anything they should or shouldn't be doing.

The committee's response was that this was just an opportunity, not a mandate. Families — however people defined them — could do whatever made sense for them.

On Family Night, the most popular activity by far was to cook and eat a meal together. Many made family favorites or dug up old family recipes. Lots of people reported the novel experience of making food from scratch. After dinner, board games were popular. Marra's family watched old family videos.

Afterward, the committee asked for evaluations. They expected about twenty-five. But of the twenty-four hundred families with kids in grades K through twelve, almost six hundred sent in responses. They were overwhelmingly positive, and 93 percent of the responders added comments to the form — some of them paragraphs long. Marra says, "People said things like, I'm surprised at how much our kids ate it up; we thought they'd be bored by it."

Since then, the organizers of Ridgewood Family Night have continued to be deluged by publicity. When I speak to Marra, on the verge of the third running of what is now an annual event, she says that, in the past week, she has received sixty-five requests for kits designed to help people start similar events in their own communities. Hasbro, the toy manufacturer, has given the group money to send out folders that include sample goal sheets, lists of lessons learned, posters, evaluations, a refrigerator magnet, as well as a brochure from Hasbro for a Family Game Night.

"It's so fascinating the requests I get," Marra says. "From Kentucky, Ohio, Michigan, Minnesota, Georgia . . . and they put little comments. People are feeling like this everywhere. They're worried that all the rushing is not the best thing for their kids. And they can connect with us. They think, *Now, here's a place to start.* It gives them hope they can change."

For his part, Rosenfeld has been promoting "National Family Night" and "Family Night A Month." According to its Web site, the purpose of the National Family Night Organization is:

- To raise national awareness about the impact of over-scheduling on families and children.
- To encourage families to examine their day-to-day schedules and to choose what matters most.
- To actively involve America's parents, educators, coaches, legislators, religious leaders and other community leaders in an on-going, nationwide dialogue about the ways our communities can foster a balance between family time, unscheduled activities, and outside enrichment activities.

These initiatives are critically important. They highlight many of the same issues we learn about when we focus on supper. When families spend an evening together, the most obvious thing for them to do is to eat. And conversely, when families eat together, they are more likely to spend time together. The way we spend our time is a window to our values. Every mark on the calendar highlights our priorities. In our highly organized, tightly scripted lives, if we don't make time for something, it's not going to happen.

So what does it mean to have a once-a-year day? Will it nestle into the national conscience like Mother's Day, or capture our imagination like Valentine's Day? Or does it become the equivalent of Secretary's Day, National Mole Day, or National Day of Puppetry? Does it give us permission to pay lip service once, and then forget about it? Or is this one night a year the harbinger of things to come?

I have not heard of any other communities following the path laid out by Wayzata and Ridgewood. But an awful lot of people seem to be interested in trying.

CAMBRIDGE, MASSACHUSETTS: EVERYTHING I LEARNED...

The city of Cambridge, Massachusetts, where I spent my young adulthood, can look like two very different towns. It is home to the cupola'd buildings of Harvard, MIT, and a prosperous colony of academic spin-offs. But this city of one hundred thousand also includes a sizable immigrant and working-class population crowded into wooden triple-deckers and squat public housing. Luckily, in 1997, when the city convened a task force on children's welfare that focused on kids most at risk, the group was able to take advantage of a research project based at the Harvard Graduate School of Education to build a creative program all its own. It isn't often that academic research has such a neighborly, direct, and positive outcome. Here is a story of Local Study Makes Good.

In the 1980s, a group of researchers based primarily at

Harvard had been interested in the link between the size of children's vocabulary and the ease with which they learned to read. Anecdotal evidence told them that kids who showed up in kindergarten knowing more words had a head start toward reading. The researchers, whom I'll call the Ed School Team, also felt that proficiency in reading would help kids later, with reading-based subjects such as history and science.

They decided to study disadvantaged kids because, as one of the researchers, Catherine Snow, explains to me, "One of the things middle-class families do, they get tutors, they bitch and complain to teachers, they get special help if the kids don't read." So middle-class kids are more likely to end up in good shape. For the purposes of the study, however, the team wanted kids whose outcomes would be more varied as they traveled through their school years.

They found eighty-three low-income families in the Boston area who had three-year-old children. The families varied by ethnicity, race, family composition, and whether or not they were on welfare. Because they wanted to test what kinds of activities might affect children's reading, the Ed School Team recorded the youngsters playing with toys and having their parents read stories to them. The researchers asked the parents lots of questions about the kids' reading and about their television viewing, the two activities they assumed would mark the poles of language acquisition (TV watching — bad; parents reading to kids — good). Then, as a matter of practicality, not because they thought it was important, they also asked the parents to tape-record the kids' family suppers. As team member Patton O. Tabors explains, "As sociolinguists, we see how language develops in a social context. The language they [the children] acquire is the language they're hearing." At supper, they could reach all the people in the child's "social context" in one fell swoop.

When the researchers listened to these recordings, they were looking for what they call decontextualized language — talk about things or ideas that are not right in front of you, that do not depend on context to be understood. Asking for the salt doesn't count, because the child could be nodding toward the salt, making the meaning apparent. They also looked for explanatory talk (*Please pass the salt because I want it for my potato*) and narrative talk, the kind that creates mini stories. Two typically kidlike examples of narrative talk can be found in the book they wrote about this research, *Beginning Literacy with Language*: "Tommy threw up orange all over the teacher," and "Remember when we went to Montreal and we crashed the car?"

When the Ed School Team tabulated the results, much to their surprise they found that, more than playing, more than being read to, supper was the place where children built vocabulary. Evidently children swallowed and digested new words and new language skills along with their noodles or chicken or pie. In the first two years of the study, the researchers recorded two thousand "rare" words. More than one thousand of them were heard at the dinner table. Only 143 came from being read to.

Snow explains that, at supper, "Kids observe adults talking to one another in a way in which they're allowed to participate. Supper is a time that's culturally constructed where the task is to chat. At other times there are likely to be other things going on." As well, because many people are gathered together, conversation gets more interesting, with more tiny stories being told, more decontextualized language, more explanations. And having more than one adult at the table presents even more opportunities for learning — yet another argument for having the whole family sit down together.

Their book includes the suppertime example of a boy named Casey, reporting that firefigters came to his school that day, and that they carried tanks on their backs. Casey's father immediately provides an explanation:

> FATHER: You know what oxygen is? That's . . .
> CASEY: Yeah, you put that, and you get air
> from it.
> FATHER: That's the air because when you go in the
> fires, you're in the fire house, smoke gets
> in, and you cough and you can't breathe.
> You can use that oxygen and get some
> fresh air in you.

When Casey refers to the oxygen being on the firefighters' backs, his father reminds him of the toy scuba diver, with a tank on his back, that Casey plays with in the bathtub. So this conversation introduces the word *oxygen*, and puts it in a context the child understands. This is the way vocabulary builds. Snow explains, "Words are not just labels; they are entry points to whole domains of knowledge." Which is why new and unusual words are so important, and why they are more likely to appear at dinner, when conversation moves back and forth, and stories are told.

This exposure to a larger vocabulary becomes critical when it's time for children to learn to read. At the most basic level, children read words. If they have to decode both the word and the meaning, it's a much more difficult task.

Knowing lots of words means also being familiar with the internal structure of words. This familiarity helps in things like standing up in front of the class at sharing time. It's the base for writing. It helps kids master subjects as they reach higher grades.

The fact that the Ed School Team was able to follow fifty of the kids through tenth grade allowed them to see how early reading success or failure played out over time. (They have remained in touch with some of the young people to this day.) Snow says, "The frequency at which they [the children] were exposed to rare words at three and four predicted their kindergarten vocabulary. We found vocabulary at kindergarten was a very good predictor of reading comprehension throughout the rest of their lives." Early success in reading breeds confidence and enhanced expectations on the part of both student and teacher. Tabors says, "There's a very strong link between kindergarten, fourth grade, ninth grade, tenth grade. It really seems to set the stage for academic success." She jokes, "At one point, we thought about calling the book *Everything I Learned I Learned Before Kindergarten.*"

By now, the kids in the study have had very different outcomes. Tabors says, "Some are in college, some have gone right from apprenticeships in technical schools to jobs; some are parents, some are just sitting on the couch at home. Some kids were held back in ninth or tenth grade; their teachers decided they were never going to make it."

Snow explains what happens when things don't work well: "Kids who are poor readers nowadays aren't going to get high school diplomas. The youngest and slowest of our kids got caught by the MCAS [Massachusetts Comprehensive Assessment System — the standardized test now required for high school graduation in Massachusetts]. You fail that test in tenth grade, then again in eleventh grade and twelfth grade, you don't get a high school diploma." Incredibly, the stage for all this may be set at the toddlers' suppers.

Of course, Tabors points out, there's always the possibility that we're looking at all of this backward: that the families who were talking more at dinner might have been interacting more effectively at other times as well. "Talking may be an indicator, not an end in itself." And nobody is saying that supper is the only time that families talk to each other. It's just that, in our culture, it is the primary one.

You can also see how a family who continues to have regular conversations might be more able to help their kids over the years. Hearing daily reports of mini failures and successes helps parents stay tuned to children's progress, and shows when they might need intervention, praise, or help. But this benefit comes after the most basic one of being well prepared to start school.

So when the Cambridge city group wanted to develop a program that would benefit all the city's children, they were so impressed by the Ed School research that they chose reading readiness as a "win-able, do-able" goal. They developed an oral language development campaign called Let's Talk . . . It Makes a Difference! (or *Hablemos . . . eso hace la diferencia!*, or *Vamos falar . . . isto faz diferenca!* or *An nou pale . . . sa fe yon diferans!*). The thinking was that, with a limited budget, the city could get long-term, broad results from improving young children's linguistic skills.

According to Lei-Anne Ellis, literacy coordinator for the Agenda for Children, "The Harvard research says that the size of a kid's vocabulary at the end of kindergarten correlates very highly to tenth-grade reading comprehension. So there's a big push these days on coming to kindergarten with an expressive vocabulary of around twenty-two hundred words." If you're going to read *The buffalo was eating the grass in the pasture*, you have to know what the words *buffalo*, *grass*, and *pasture* mean. Otherwise, it's double-processing. If kids have a large vocabulary, when they encounter the word in print, they're less thrown. Ellis says, "Our everyday conversations are the trampoline to book language. Oral language is simpler, but we need to know that simpler language to understand the more complex."

She says that, by improving their spoken language, children also expand their grammar. A small child will say, *I goed to the park with Mommy.* When that child learns that's not how we do it in English, he will internalize the grammatical structure. In addition, children build up a reservoir of understanding, of background knowledge and ideas. Also, Ellis, says, "We felt that it was a message that we could give no matter what your level of education was, what your language was" — an important factor in a city that, ethnically and economically speaking, is all over the map.

The program, which is funded with a combination of city, state, and federal money, has been running now for two years. It helps parents understand that they should talk to their children, and it also helps them learn how to make that talk richer. They are encouraged to use past, present, and future tenses, and to have children expand their conversations by talking about things other than what is right in front of them. The Let's Talk folks strongly recommend talking at supper, where there is an obvious opportunity for vocabulary-building conversations.

An important part of the program is encouraging non-English-speaking parents to speak to their children in their native language. Some immigrant parents, because they want their children to get ahead, only speak to them in English. But that can limit their conversations, as well as the child's grasp of language, period. It can also do serious damage to the parent–child relationship. Ellis tells me about high school students who complain to the guidance officers in tears that they cannot speak to their parents. They are not saying that their parents don't appreciate them. They are saying that they literally cannot understand each other, because their parents speak only Spanish, or Ethiopian, or Creole, while the children speak only English.

As Snow, the Harvard sociolinguist, explains, even if children learn one language at home and then have to learn English when they go to school, it will be easier to learn the second language if they have a richer first language: "They don't have to build a whole new set of concepts — just attach a new word to the old concept." Besides, she says, "What's the point of talking less, or in a way that's more impoverished or less interesting?"

The Cambridge program also empowers the parents, no matter what their background or level of education. It can only improve the parent–child relationship, while it strengthens the child's link to her cultural background. From what I've now learned about childhood resilience, this can only help children to cope in the world.

And it all happens most naturally at supper. Ellis says, "Supper is the time when, if they sit down with the kids, the families have at least twenty minutes; everyone is together (if they're not watching TV). You can have these extended conversations. You can have three or four conversations, or ten conversations, because people are not preoccupied with folding socks or doing other chores; the connection is there; the opportunity is there. It's the length of time, and the fact that parents can concentrate. There's something about breaking bread in many cultures; when you break the bread together, it's a sign of peace. Everyone tries a little bit to make it work; it's less hostile than Have you done your homework?"

The Let's Talk people give out goodies — tote bags and bibs and sippy-cups — with their motto. They have colorful placards available in several languages aimed at parents with a low level of literacy: LET'S TALK . . . BECAUSE — THAT IS HOW A BABY LEARNS TO TALK — THAT IS HOW A TODDLER LEARNS LOTS OF NEW WORDS — THAT IS HOW A PRESCHOOL CHILD LEARNS ALL ABOUT THE WORLD THEY LIVE IN — A CHILD WITH LOTS OF EARLY EXPERIENCE TALKING AND LISTENING WILL EASILY LEARN TO READ AND WRITE. IT MAKES A DIFFERENCE!

Ellis tells me a bit about her own supper history. She grew up in Hawaii, in a family of Chinese and Hawaiian origin. English was her mother's third language, which she did not learn until she went to school. "If you had said to her, Talk to your children, you might as well say, Jump out the window." When Ellis was ten, her family opened a restaurant. Sometimes they ate together before they served the evening meal, but mostly they caught bites separately while they worked.

Now she has three children, two of whom are out of the house. But they still come home and eat. "Meals are very important to us. When everyone is there, meals go on and on. Our meals now are full of conversation."

THE UNITED STATES: FAMILY DAY KICK-OFF

I am in the wood-paneled conference room of the Henry J. Kaiser Family Foundation in Washington, D.C., for the launch of the 2003 Family Day: A Day to Eat Dinner with Your Family. The room is full of suits. My press kit contains a copy of the Family Day poster: very horizontal and narrow, shaped to fit on the sides of city buses and the insides of subway cars. ONE HABIT THAT PREVENTS ANOTHER, it says. On the left is a picture of a family eating together. The family and the style of the photo are energetic and casual; we don't see the father's head at all. On the right, someone is smoking a joint. The subtitle: THE MORE OFTEN KIDS EAT DINNER WITH THEIR FAMILIES, THE LESS LIKELY THEY ARE TO SMOKE, DRINK, OR USE ILLEGAL DRUGS.

It's an okay poster, not great, but this is a complicated (read: two-part) message that must be difficult to convey. Even though I know that Family Day, the fourth Monday in September, comes with a presidential proclamation and is officially endorsed by the governors of more than half the states as well as dozens of organizations ranging from the AFL-CIO, the Central Conference of American Rabbis, and the National Council of Churches down to the National Tabletop and Giftware Association, it has the unmistakable second-tier feel of a do-good organization, the curse of the nonprofit in a for-profit world.

Family Day is a project of CASA, the National Center on Addiction and Substance Abuse at Columbia University. It was their research on the importance of family suppers that had first shocked me into finding out more about this topic. Its president, Joseph A. Califano Jr., is the first speaker. Pink faced, gray haired, and enthusiastic, he carries an echo of New York in his voice. Family Day began in 2001, he tells the audience, but it is getting more muscle each year. Coke is the sponsor for the second year; General Mills has signed on for three years as presenting sponsor. The big news this year is the addition of public service announcements starring Jamie Lee Curtis, Barbara Bush, and her son, the president. I, cynically, think that using the Bushes as a poster family for how to avoid drug and alcohol problems may be pushing it.

CASA's first two goals are to "Inform Americans of the economic and social costs of substance abuse and its impact on their lives," and to "Assess what works in prevention, treatment, and law enforcement." The organization has been involved in a broad range of research and programs involving ex-offenders, ex-addicts, and women on welfare. But Family Day has the potential to cut across all categories. All of us eat, don't we?

Califano tells us the dinner project is a "national effort to promote parental engagement; a way to talk and listen to their kids, help raise healthier children." He reviews the ways that drugs have a destructive impact throughout society. Describing the importance of getting our youngsters through their teenage years without using drugs, he asks the million-dollar question: "How do you get that child through age twenty-one?" His answer: "It is family, family, family." This optimistic yet practical message is not lost on the audience of reporters and social service types. It is so refreshing to hear a note of hope.

The next speaker, Arthur T. Dean, chairman and CEO of the Community Anti-Drug Coalitions of America, is a retired general. He gets us into the particulars, running through a long list of homegrown programs: The Greater Williamsburg, Virginia, County Park and Rec will cancel evening activities in honor of Family Day. Twenty restaurants in the Williamsburg area are giving discounts to family groups. Frankfort, Kentucky, is hosting a lunch with local children, their parents, the governor and his spouse.

I think: *None of these things is large, but maybe taken together they will have an impact.* I think: *It takes years and years and years for this type of program to build.* Public awareness increases one person at a time. It takes a lot of park and rec cancellations, a lot of governors' luncheons, to reach a critical mass.

Next up is Wade Horn, PhD, assistant secretary for children and families in the U.S. Department of Health and Human Services, a former president of the National Fatherhood Initiative. He is beaming with enthusiasm. "We know that kids who have good relations with their parents are less likely to engage in risky behaviors," he says. "To have a good relationship requires time. But spending time is not enough. Something else has to go into this connection — a context that's positive."

Horn tells us about his own childhood, as one of seven children. "The rule was, we eat dinner together unless there's a once-in-a-lifetime event." He tells us about the time, years ago, when he brought his then-girlfriend, now-wife home for supper. "We sat down at seven o'clock. At ten-thirty she nudged me: 'Doesn't your family ever leave the dinner table?'"

Then Califano shows us the public service announcements (PSAs) that will run on radio and TV. The first spot features President Bush and his mother. It begins with a woman's voice, off camera, speaking to George W., who appears to be taking questions from a crowd.

"Mr. President, did you and your family eat dinner together when you were growing up?"

President Bush says, "Yes, unless Mother was cooking."

We cut to a close-up of Barbara Bush, wearing a suit and a flag pin. "It's not good making fun of your mother, even if you are president," she says.

Several very posed-looking photos of the Bush family over the years appear as she continues: "But it *is* good to have dinner with your kids a lot. We know that the more often children have dinner with their families, the less likely they are to smoke, drink, and use drugs. And getting to age twenty-one that way means they likely never will. So, simply having dinner together can help your kids forever."

Then she gives us the punchline: "Even if you're not a great cook."

Next comes a radio spot in which Jamie Lee Curtis invites families to eat supper "not at my house; at yours." The spots are funny, but stilted in a PSA way. We are told that they will run on TV and radio; related slides will be shown on movie screens for a month, and posters will run on buses and subways in nine major cities.

It's time to wrap up. "Please, please stay with this," Califano exhorts us. "We're going to make this one of the most important days in America."

The do-gooder, optimistic mother in me says Yeah! I am in on the beginning! This is so important! But the jaded journalist part of me answers, Oh sure, you and what army? Even *with* Barbara Bush, you know very well how easy it is for audiences to tune out PSAs. What chance does a ten-second spot have against the daily media deluge, or the imperatives of career, of self-improvement, of exhaustion? Plus, who *wants* to show up to a house full of needy people when you're dog tired and just want to have a good walk, a chat with a friend, or a long cooling drink? When your teenager is wailing that you're ruining her life by making her sit through yet another family supper, who can remember that she actually means just the opposite? Who can keep believing that the most important thing we can do as parents is to be there, night after night after night?

As the meeting breaks up, I am still curious about how CASA came up with its initial results. When they ran the first survey, had they expected dinner to be so important? I ask Califano about the study's beginnings, and he confirms that the results were "serendipitous." He then returns to the question of what teenagers want and need compared with what they say: "We do a lot of focus groups with children. Especially with two parents working, they see [parents] making dinner as an expression of caring about them, being engaged in their lives. Teenagers complain about curfews. But you get them in focus groups, they say, My parents really care about me."

There are three weeks between the launch and Family Day. During that time, as I go about my life in one of the major cities on the CASA publicity list, I see nothing in the newspapers, hear nothing on the radio. I see nothing on television or at the movies, no ads on the buses or in the subways. I call the multiplex nearest my house, which is owned by National Amusements, and ask the manager if he's running the Family Day slide. "I never heard of Family Day," he tells me, and gives me the phone number for what he calls Corporate. A day later, the National Amusements spokesperson calls to let me know that they're running the Family Day slide in all their fourteen Massachusetts theaters, but only until three days before Family Day. So someone at Corporate is short-changing the commitment. And the local theater manager hasn't even heard of the idea, let alone been impressed with the buzz.

On the actual Family Day, a friend tells me the event has earned a mention on CNN. I also find a story in *Parade* magazine. So that's really good; the publicity machine *is* kicking in. The *Parade* story runs in the "Fresh Voices" column, and it's headed, DINNER IS OUR PEACEFUL TIME. Half a dozen teens describe dinner at their house.

Seventeen-year-old Spencer says, "On Friday or Saturday nights, we have 'drive-in' dinner, with hamburgers, chili dogs or my favorite, Frito pies. We eat in front of the TV, watching a movie, with the tablecloth on the floor like a picnic."

Eighteen-year-old Tracey says, "My mom cooks at about 7:30, so we eat then, but we don't eat together at the table. My mom and stepdad take their food in their room, and my sister and brother and I eat in the living room and watch TV. We don't say much. Sometimes I come home so tired from basketball practice that I just fall asleep and have leftovers later. Everyone has their own habit of going separate ways and eating."

Sixteen-year-old Jon says, "My parents work ungodly hours. And during the summer, I had three jobs, and my sister had two — so we were hardly ever home at the same time to eat together. Now we sometimes just make our own meals and eat alone. But every chance we get, we try to eat a family meal. Dinner is our peaceful time."

I'm not sure if this is good news or bad, although I'm leaning heavily toward the latter. *Parade* is a great national forum. But look at what's out there: The highlight of Spencer's family's week is TV and Frito pie. Hey, it's better than the family whose parents retreat to their room, a sce-nario I try to imagine. Do they shut the door behind them? Spread the food out on top of their bedspread while they sit cross-legged on the bed, trying not to spill their drinks? More likely it's TV and TV trays. Do they at least talk to each other? Do they dislike their kids so much they can't bear to be with them, or are they just so desperate for a little quiet, a little together time?

And what will happen when Barbara Bush wags her finger at them? Will they rush out of their room, vowing to do better for their offspring? Will they all eat together the next night? And the next?

I know that putting this subject on the table, as it were, is a good beginning, but it is only that. We will need many more Family Days if we want this message to reach all the cities and towns out beyond even Wayzata and Ridgewood.

Making It Better

In the Kitchen

AND SO WE come to the *Think globally, act locally* part of the program. Although we can go on about mores, values, sociological patterns, and spiritual depths, we all know that, first and foremost, supper is about eating. So, again: Make it worth coming to the table. If franks and beans does it for you, then by all means, open that can with a glad heart. If only your grandmother's recipe or the latest gourmet/nutritional delicacy gets your juices going, then spend whatever time you can peel off from the rest of your life to get that dish marinated, diced, sautéed, grilled, baked, artfully plated, and served. If you are a creative type, then fire wildly away. If you're a recipe follower, get out those measuring spoons and level off each one with a knife.

I enjoy lots of things about cooking — the physical activity of mixing and kneading and slicing, the sense that I can produce something that will make my loved ones happy, the control it gives me over how much I am spending, what is going into my food, how much I am producing.

Let's take lemons. I always find it amazing that, if I get it into my head that I want to have, say, a lemon meringue pie, as long as I'm willing to invest the time, I can produce one. It may not have the starched good looks of the store-bought version, but it has a taste that makes you think, *Oh now, this is what that store-bought version dreams of being.* If I decide that I'd like a bowl of that tangy egg-lemon soup I've tried at a Greek restaurant, I can come up with a reasonable facsimile. I have made fresh lemonade (puts even the best commercial preparation to shame). I have made, and used, preserved lemons. (These are strangely great, and keep in the fridge for months, sparkling up an otherwise boring dish when nothing else is around.) I have made an improbable side dish that uses lemon Jell-O and canned tomatoes that is delicious and simple.

Increasingly, though, people like me are in the minority. For some reason, we act as if these homey skills were either too high above us or too far below us; too difficult to master even as they are too boring to even merit our consideration. We devalue the competent home cook while elevating the professional chef to star status. I'm guessing that the reasons have to do with our collective amnesia around what used to be called the household arts, the specialization of everything, the professional progress of women, the outsourcing of parenthood, the economics of food production, the cult of celebrity. The results are enormous kitchens that are full of equipment but lacking in the happy disorder of productive daily life. The human results are people who, when they're hungry for supper, like the old Jewish-princess joke, can make only one thing — reservations.

To me, that seems really sad. What if you're sick and don't want to go out? What if you have a child, or a spouse, who just wants something really, really plain? What if you want to sit around and talk, eat, and hang out with friends? If you're on a budget, if you've got health concerns, if you live in a place where the restaurants are sparse, crummy, crowded, expensive, or all of the above, you will serve yourself best (pun intended) by making sure your culinary skills are up to par — *par* being a standard defined by you. And don't tell me you'll just heat up individual frozen entrées. Where is the primal warmth in that?

In the kitchen, as in other areas of life, you should glory in your strengths and shore up your weaknesses, although I would recommend acquiring a baseline level of competence and comfort. Do you know which ingredients go with which others? Have you got some command of knives, utensils, pots, pans, ovens, broilers, and stoves? Can you balance a meal in terms of food groups, flavor, texture, difficulty of preparation? If not, learn however you learn best: through books, newspapers, TV, adult ed classes, phone calls to Mom, or just hanging out with a friend who's better at it than you.

Make sure your kitchen is stocked with necessities — a couple of good, sharp knives, some mixing bowls, frying pans, sturdy food-storage containers, a cutting board. Any implement or machine that only does one thing is a space waster in my book, although I'll make an exception for the ergonomic vegetable peeler.

If you plan to have your kids help out, get extra measuring cups, mixing bowls, wooden spoons, and the aforementioned peelers. Lynn Fredericks suggests giving each child his own set of equipment that gets stored in that child's special place. (Before you start grousing about space, remember that she lives in a New York apartment.)

But here's how you can help yourself right away: Take stock of which resources you can muster in your environment — prepared foods, take-out, made-ahead homemade dishes, leftovers. Be aware of which human resources you can entice or manhandle into doing more of the work (read: spouse, children, any other available warm bodies). And don't forget my kitchen rules: (1) The cook gets to make what she likes. (2) The cook gets to choose which jobs she wants to do. (3) Never underestimate the amount of guilt produced as a by-product of cooking. If you prepare the meal, you can often get someone else to clean up.

Be aware of where you stand on the planning–spontaneity axis. If you are the organized type, or aspire to become more organized, plan out your menus for the week and shop accordingly. Then combine as much of the prep work as is feasible: Sauté enough onions or garlic, chop enough parsley, cook enough rice to last you the week. If you're not that organized, then think about cooking double the amount you need for one night and banking the rest.

You may notice that this section is heavily weighted toward the Mommy-making-food-every-night model. That's what's worked in my marriage and my family, but as I've said often, you should do what gives strength, pleasure, and meaning to your particular clan. Just do it with intention and gusto.

When you put meals together, alternate colors and textures. If you realize that you are, unwittingly, in the midst of producing an all-white meal, sprinkle the potatoes (say) with chopped parsley, and the fish (say) with paprika. It adds a bit of flavor and improves the look dramatically. My mother learned this in nursing school in the 1930s, when she was preparing meals that would appeal to people who had lost their appetite. If I had to name my top magic ingredient, it would still be paprika.

Learn which spices and flavorings go together: the soy-ginger-hoisin-garlic route; the butter-white-wine tack; the chili-sour-cream-raw-onion connection; the sweet-and-sour combo of balsamic vinegar and brown sugar; something sweet like dried fruits paired with capers or olives. I realize that, with some of these flavorings, we're heading into dangerous territory. On the one hand, I want to say, Don't be tyrannized by the neophobia of your children; you do them no favors by assuming they can't eat real food. On the other hand, I want to let you know that you can cook your dish plain and pour the sauce over it at the end.

If you're a real beginner, I suggest finding one meal and getting comfortable with it. Spaghetti with meat sauce, salad, and garlic bread was the standard first dinner of my friends when I was in first-apartment days, although a lot of times the garlic bread was too daunting. When you can whip up your signature dish anytime you want, you'll get bored and begin to branch out, although, if you don't want to, you don't have to go very far. Some of the best home cooks have a very limited repertoire.

I am the opposite — always looking for something new to make for supper. And yes, that means presenting dishes that flop, but I consider this a reasonable price to pay for a lifetime of culinary adventure. With time, you do get better at reading a recipe and making a guess about whether or not it will work for you. (Bonus advice: Steer clear of turkey meat loaf. It is always too dry.)

Still, I never want to commit to a lot of time or effort to a weekday meal. And I am not a big menu planner. While I always stock my pantry with basic items, I also enjoy the rush that comes from opening up the vegetable bin at the last possible moment, taking stock of the contents — sorry-looking carrot, brown leathery orange, wilted parsley — and figuring out what I can do. If you are the type who can lay out your week's worth of meals, buy all the ingredients in one massive supermarket trip, and then move through your plan and your cupboard in an orderly fashion as your week unfolds, you don't need my congratulations or my advice; you're already well ahead of any game I've ever played. While it is satisfying to work with a full deck, it is also fun to pull off the hat trick required when you have nothing but a growling stomach, a cranky baby, and a ticking clock.

I do know what I need to get by, though, and I strongly suggest that you figure out what *getting by* means for you. In my house, this has varied over the years, but the longest-running standard is some kind of egg dish. Over time, the eggs have been prepared with: tiny jars of cheap pretend red caviar and sour cream, or cheddar cheese, or ratatouille, or turkey bacon, or pretend meats made out of tofu, or feta cheese and tomatoes. Salami and eggs made pancake style (use oil, not butter) and slathered with mustard was one of my mother's best fallbacks ever.

I always have rice, pasta, canned tuna, canned tomatoes, canned salmon, canned clams, canned anchovies, canned corn, as well as walnuts and pignolia nuts. I also try to always have garlic, onions, parsley, lemon, apple, orange, and maybe a dried old piece of Parmesan. There is usually some kind of vegetable lying around, maybe in a pathetic state, but we are talking basic. I also always have canned soups, mostly broth, as well as canned pumpkin and some peanut butter. My basic basic includes a full range of spices, as well as things like soy sauce, hoisin, fish sauce, balsamic vinegar, good olive oil, butter, a healthful vegetable oil, Worcestershire sauce, horseradish, and a jar of chutney. From these, I work my two-bit magic.

You may notice that I'm not big on frozen foods, although

when my kids were young and ravenous my basics included frozen French bread pizzas. (Remember how I dissed them back in chapter 1? When you actually have to get supper on the table every night, snobbery will get you nowhere.)

My pantry always holds a can or two of salmon, because salmon patties were a cheap staple in my mother's Depression-era childhood, and they remained a constant in mine. Salmon patties are probably the same idea as crabcakes, which I have never tasted. Crabs are not kosher because they are shellfish. Although my family has not kept kosher for two generations, food habits die hard. I eat lots of nonkosher foods, but I could tell you when I first tasted every one.

Your own fallback list will reflect your particular climate, ethnic heritage, social class, and level of interest in nutrition. It should be able to carry you through the nights when you have no time and no reserves of invention or good humor; when all you want for supper is an aspirin, a drink, or a fairy godmother. I can remember, as a small child, eating, and truly enjoying, a piece of bread broken up in a bowl of milk, but if you were to suggest that to me now, I would be hard-pressed to remain civil.

So here's what you do on those miserable nights. You make a decision: olive oil or butter. You cut up an onion. You sauté. This buys you a couple of minutes to think: Italian? Pseudo-French? Semi-Chinese? Texish-Mexish? In the meantime, the kitchen is filling with bright comforting smells. The pan is sizzling. You can start yelling at the kids to set the table. The family knows that you are hard at work, that you care about them, and that something will show up on the table soon. In the meantime, if the kids are howling-hungry, toss them a bunch of carrots and something you tell them is a dip. This can be salsa, or yogurt mixed with anything, or maybe peanut butter or processed cheese. Think *veg-and-protein*. Or put them to work washing lettuce or slicing cukes or green peppers or apples or bananas. They're less apt to whine if they are part of the team, and you can always add the products of their labor to your completed dish as a garnish. A toddler, wearing an apron, can "wash" a few plastic containers and utensils in the sink. An infant can sit on the floor, or in the playpen, and bang said utensils, or a nice pot top, making a satisfying noise. A frail or old person can read the paper to you while you work. That's why I much prefer a kitchen table to a counter. You can lean back and get comfortable. It gives a homier feel.

The best kitchen I know belongs to my friend Patience, and has a fireplace, two wing chairs, and just enough clutter. But that may be pushing it. In your world, comfort might be better defined by a working air conditioner. Even a minuscule galley kitchen can accommodate a folding step stool. The point is to make the food-preparation area welcoming, to encourage the hanging around that is often a precursor to helping out. It's common knowledge that, at a party, no matter how big the house, everyone gravitates to the kitchen. When we turn our back on family suppers, we are throwing away that natural human draw.

If time is not on your side at the suppertime witching hour, then analyze your time in its entirety. (Don't laugh.) Throw some sweet potatoes in the oven as you sit down to dinner. They will allow you to start out a step ahead tomorrow. Even though you're not able to do the two-hour-slow-cooking thing in the late afternoon, you may well be able to squeeze it in over the weekend, or in the evening after supper is done. Slow-cooking doesn't mean you have to be standing there watching the pot every second. Usually, just checking on it every half hour, giving it a stir and a bit more hot water if necessary, is enough. Our ancestors lived on hearty meals like chicken soups, vegetable soups, fish chowders, pot roasts, and New England boiled dinners for a reason — on a cold winter night, they are cheap, they are nutritious, and they make you feel damned good. If it's hot out, make a summer soup in the evening, then leave it overnight in the fridge. Slap together a sandwich the next night, and you've got yourself a meal. Or, if you thrive on last-minute decisions and crave freshness, you might think about how your day unfolds. There may be enough time for you to pop into the store and pick up your last-minute requirements. Drive around with an insulated container in your car if it makes you feel better.

Perhaps because I grew up visiting the butcher, the bakery, the fruit and vegetable man, the appetizing store, with my mother, I love dashing into my local stores at the end of the day, seeing what appeals to me, meeting my neighbors at Crosby's, seeing what Mary has on hand at Go Fish! If I haven't had time to shop, I actually enjoy the creative ferment of facing a refrigerator that contains a couple of stalks of leftover broccoli and the remains of last night's chicken, and figuring out what I am going to do about it. It's my own personal limbo pole: How low can I go and still produce something that looks like a meal?

I realize that for those of you who have followed Rosalie Harrington's wonderful advice and stocked your freezer with serving-sized plastic bags of delectable goodies, this will all be moot. My freezer has none of those goodies, but it does have lots of plastic containers of homemade tomato sauce. They represent the amount of time I gained when my children grew up and moved out of the house.

Did I mention how helpful it is to name what you're cooking? A personal connection is good, exotic is helpful, something that sounds appetizing wins points. Don't worry about how ridiculous the names appear. Your family may laugh at you, but they will remember. Next time, they will request the item by name. Soon, they will be describing it lovingly to their friends: Jennie's Meat Loaf. Romagnoli Pasta. Bangers and Mash. Perfection Salad. Green Eggs, No Ham.

Your children will also be interested in knowing what foods you enjoyed when you were their age. Some of these standards will still be perfectly delectable, some passable, others will probably make you gag. You can have your kids interview your own parents about suppertimes, and then put together a recipe book. Of course you will want to try out these recipes together.

Another cooking idea: Form a co-op with a couple of other families. Then you only have to cook one large meal once a week. This can be organized in your neighborhood or work group. The main dish, divided into family-sized portions, can be brought into work in the morning and stored in the company refrigerator for the day. This obviously requires coordination, and compatibility of taste and budget, but some families find it a godsend.

Don't forget presentation — by which I mean something that takes an extra two to ten seconds. Lay the food out nicely on the plate rather than dumping it into the bowl. Use your pretty stuff — what's the point of saving it for once or twice a year? My mother, dashing in fifteen minutes before my father's supper had to be on the table if he was to make his evening office hours, still ran a fork down the sides of the cucumber after it was peeled, giving the slices a scalloped effect. And why not? Isn't scalloped more fun than plain?

Encourage your kids to be part of the beautification team. Let them do the cucumber scalloping. Have them make place mats — decorating a piece of paper that you can laminate. Encourage them to take turns producing a centerpiece. This could be a LEGO construction, a favorite small doll or car, a flower, a bouquet of leaves. To repeat: Children are less likely to complain about something they've been part of. A joint effort, a shared experience, remains the goal. And try not to get bogged down by sibling rivalry. Make charts, divide up tasks, spin a pointer around a wheel.

When the researchers get out their questionnaires, assessing the high points of childhood, they find that the things kids remember with wistful affection are not the big-ticket items — vacations, pro sports games, Broadway shows — but rather the silly, oddball, throwaway things that parents and kids do together. Learn, and then show your kids how to cut a radish so it turns into a flower. While you are cooking, have your child make carrot-stick men with raisins for eyes. Let your kids string the snow peas, tear the lettuce, wash the fruit. Talk to your kids — and listen to them— while you're boiling the pasta, then let them slurp a single strand to see if it's done. Quality time is what sneaks up on you when you're looking the other way. Remember my father, contemplating his plate of Jersey tomatoes and breathing out, "This is living!"

IN THE FAMILY

As the earth moves on its axis, families all over the world watch the day come to an end. The first American families who notice are on the eastern tip of Maine. Then the sun, and the clock, move westward, to Illinois, Montana, California, and Hawaii. Families follow suit in Australia, India, Africa, and Europe before the end-of-day marker reaches our shores once again. Most families demarcate, and celebrate, this daily occurrence by joining with loved ones to share a meal. Humans have been eating together since we were cave dwellers, if not before.

If we have forgotten about this small daily sacrament, it has only been for the smallest blip of human history. And so we can lay claim to it again. No one is asking for rocket science here, only shared mac-and-cheese and a bunch of chairs pulled up around the table. There are a thousand different ways to do this. As I've said before, every family's supper will be different, except that, in some deep emotional way, each family's meal will be much the same.

Although I have had family suppers consistently throughout my entire life, I have pretty much done it by rote — because that was the way my family always did it, because I was too lazy or too dense to consider doing anything else. Now, working on this project, I have become more conscious, more likely to press for a home-cooked over a restaurant meal. I get a wonderful feeling when everyone is sitting together. (This may have something to do with the fact that my kids are grown, and have turned out well, so that seeing them has changed from being a constant to being a treat.) I'd like to think that, even if they were still little and yanking at my hair, I would have a bit more appreciation of this moment in time, although I may be flattering myself. But I do understand more of what my grandmother was about when, at large family dinners, in between the main course and the dessert, if we looked over at her (immigrant, survivor of pogroms, sole support of her children during decades of hard times) we could pretty much count on seeing her pull out her handkerchief and dab at her eye.

"What's wrong, Ma?" Her grown children would be up and worrying.

"I'm crying because I'm happy!" she would announce enthusiastically. "We're all here together."

Tears of gratitude are not necessary on a nightly basis. In reality, lots of nights the goal is only to make it through. So, while I am putting this all in a cosmic perspective, I also want to say the opposite: *Don't expect too much. Perfection is the enemy of the good. Your kids are never going to learn to . . .* (Fill in the blank. The thing they will never learn to do will change year by year.) If you have an image of some ideal supper in your mind, the only thing you can be certain of is that tonight's will not measure up.

Still, something will happen. The surface will look shaggy, but underneath, over time, a form begins to takes shape. Some type of ritual will grow. That overarching ritual, and the dozens of tiny ones that compose it, will belong to your family, and to them alone. It will give meaning, frame, boundaries, comfort.

But how to do it? Simply creating the right atmosphere can go a long way. My friend Alice, whose offspring are just emerging from the of miasma of adolescence, says, "Sometimes, when everybody sits down and looks like they're ready to kill, I decide it's up to me to say that stupid cliché stuff. (*It's great to all be together. We are so lucky to be here.*) Sometimes I do it with not the kindest of motives, but only to set the tone. But after I do, I find that it's hard to be downright nasty."

The right tone will do little, however, if your family is not there. The first step in your house may simply be getting them to come to the table together. You might start by coordinating with a special event — a birthday, holiday, or the visit of a relative or friend. If that seems scary, invite a guest or guests to help you ease into it. Then, when you've done it once, you can sneak up and do it again. Remember the advice of anthropologist Bradd Shore, that rituals might at first appear arbitrary to the kids — "but once they do it three or four times, they become quite attached to it." Do keep it positive, though.

My friends Kate and Andy raised five daughters in their blended family. During the girls' teenage years, when both parents were working, each daughter was responsible for making supper one weekday night. Some of the girls took to their jobs with enthusiastic creativity, producing ambitious and varied repasts. Monique, however, made tacos exactly the same way every Tuesday night. Literally. For years. But because Kate and Andy wanted this enterprise to succeed (indeed; they really needed to be able to depend on the girls), they ate tacos once a week, and they smiled.

Giving your children real responsibility can be tricky, but over time most kids will thrive on such a diet. And yes, expecting them to do their small jobs can look like more trouble than it's worth, but the tasks will become habit, then a source of (grudging) pride, although you should not count on being alive to witness this. Even more than specific skills, kids learn to take pride in contributing to the family enterprise. And they learn real skills. Anna Kovel, who has cooked at several of the country's top restaurants — from the iconic Chez Panisse in Berkeley to a megastylish New York boutique where the cooks were kept on display in a sort of glass box — remembers the time when she was twelve or thirteen and living with her father. When he insisted on eating "family dinners," she objected that it was just the two of them, and that she'd rather be out playing with her friends. But when he would call her up from work and tell her how to put the chicken in the oven, she remembers feeling empowered by her chicken-cooking skills.

Maybe you hesitate to institute or regularize suppers because you fear that your meal will never be As Good As It Used To Be — some misty vision of calm togetherness. But you can do better than that; you can set the stage for the kinds of meals that are useful, and deeply satisfying, right now. Use the past as inspiration or as a treasure house you can plunder. It should not be your destination.

If you are already having family meals, you will probably want to become more intentional about them, to make them a priority. The more you are aware of the value of what you have, the more you will be willing to work to maintain or expand it.

And can I please, one last time, bring up the subject of the TV? When disinviting that attention sump, let your loved ones know why you are doing it — that you care more about them than about the pretend people inside the box. Lots of families use the dinner tape ploy: When kids say they can't come to the table because they will miss their favorite show, offer to tape or TiVo it for later viewing.

Above all, be kind to yourself. Give yourself time: immediate time so that you can enjoy each other, and recurring time so that these habits can gel; so that your mealtimes have the important element of predictability. Time is our currency, time expresses our values. You may look at your daily routines as being dictated by circumstance, but be on the lookout for ways to tweak or change routines to further your long-term goals for your family.

Supper is not a cure-all. The dark forces in troubled families are not going to be excised by sharing a six o'clock meal, no matter how tasty the main course. But being assured of a dependable get-together can be a beginning. It can set the stage for a more satisfying interaction when and if the family is ready for change. In the meantime, it might help to remember the idea about manners being civilization writ small. Acting decently toward each other on a regular basis does help.

Contemporary American families need all the help we can get. Because of our glorification of the individual, our families build in the seeds of their own destruction. Compared with other cultures we have few, and tenuous, ties with extended family. As anthropologist Bradd Shore points out, unless we work in a family business or share a family vacation house, we are not likely to depend on each other in any significant way. In our small nuclear families, we feature separate bedrooms. We encourage children to go out on sleepovers, or to camp. We celebrate each step that attenuates our ties. The successful child is the one who has moved away from home. We should, therefore, privilege those ways that bring us together, no matter how ordinary, how modest. Supper is one of the few rituals that allow us to act out our concern for each other, our need and desire to be together.

Supper celebrates our being together, making and marking the transition from work to home, from day to night, from public to private. To increase the effectiveness of your own supper rituals, be aware of how your meal begins and ends. Wait until everyone is at the table. Say a prayer, or just go around the table and say something you're grateful for this day. Light candles, or change the lighting in the room. Make a toast. Wait until everyone has been served before you begin to eat.

At the end of the meal, reverse what you did in the beginning. Blow out the candles. Say an after-dinner prayer. Thank the cook. Thank the people who helped prepare/serve/clean up. Thank everyone for being together. (This may be particularly helpful with teenagers, who are immersed in their own busy lives.) Some families expect children to ask to be excused if they are finished before the others. I think this is a reflection of the inherently social nature of the event. It is why being sent away from the table constitutes a punishment. A meal is something we undertake together.

What should you make for supper? An adventure, a party, a lifeline; a quiet space in a busy day. Come to the table famished. Leave it feeling deliciously filled.

BEYOND YOUR FOUR WALLS

I hope I have given you a glimpse of how family supper can work its magic inside your home. But I don't have to tell you that, once you step out your front door, the pressures of the world are waiting, varied and massed. I have included some ways to respond to them. But it has taken us the better part of a generation to significantly weaken the institution of family supper, and it is going to take time, consciousness, and concerted effort to effect meaningful change. You, however, have already begun. The first step toward change is awareness.

When you enjoy suppers as a family, you will notice the factors that impinge on this enjoyment. You will see the areas where you can push back, making your schedule, and your family, more supper friendly. The smallest changes involve personal habits. Take a good look at your whole week's schedule and see what can be shifted, what can be let go. Be aware of which parts of your day are productive and which you use for downtime. It might make sense for you to squeeze in activities that don't require a lot of mental work, like exercise or grocery shopping, at the margins of the day, early in the morning, late at night, the odd times on weekends. Take advantage of our 24/7 world. Next, take a hard look at the time wasters — TV and computers, but also the automatic extracurriculars. Try to separate your own sense of insecurity from an honest assessment of what will help your family now, and in the future. And yes, this is the hard part. If you need bucking up, go back and look at the chapter about Putting Family First. Or check out their Web site. Above all, talk this over with family and friends. You are not alone.

In addition to learning to say no to nonessential activities for your children and yourself, you will want to say no in a more public way. Complain when events are scheduled at suppertime. Start petitions. Speak to schedulers. You are not the only person who has this problem. You are not the only person who cares about the continuing erosion of family life. What is really important? Listen to your heart.

A statement issued by the Admissions Department of Harvard College in 2001 lamented that: "It is common to encounter even the most successful students, who have won all the 'prizes,' stepping back and wondering if it was all worth it. Professionals in their thirties and forties — physicians, lawyers, academics, business people, and others — sometimes give the impression that they are dazed survivors of some bewildering life-long boot-camp." Their prescription? "Families should allow for more 'down-time' during vacations, weekends, and during the week at mealtimes or at any other break in the action. . . ."

Give yourself more credit. One of the sad things revealed by Ridgewood's Family Night is the way some parents worried that their children would be bored by spending an evening at home with their family. You do not have to be wealthy, a genius, or any kind of extraordinary person to provide a satisfying and warm home life. Your family does not want someone extraordinary. They want each other.

We hear a lot of that rather odd phrase *Being there for someone*, which I suppose means that you can count on the person when you are in need. But how can you be there for someone if you aren't even there? Parents today are under extreme pressure from all sides. Carving out what Wendy Mogel referred to as a little holy place, a small sacred time, can be a lifesaver.

The next set of ripples out beyond your own supper table, your own house, is your peers. Talk this issue up among your friends and colleagues. Find like-minded families. If you have kids, find families with children older than yours. Find families who are farther along on this specturm. See how they do it.

Arrange a lecture by an expert or a discussion night for parents at your local school. Then build on the interest that this generates. Get other community members on board. Take advantage of the organizations that already exist in your town. Don't rush to put on a public event before you are pretty sure about what that event should be, and why you should commit to it.

William Doherty, who helped get the Wayzata group off the ground, suggests that, at least in the beginning, you spend more time in planning and less on acting. "You go for at least eight months with the leadership group before you choose your action steps," he suggests. Then he adds, "That is hard for Americans." We want quick fixes. During that formative period, he explains, "The group is congealing. They're drafting a mission statement, choosing a name for the project, generating a variety of action steps, talking to friends and neighbors. It should be a very deliberate, democratic process."

Once you have located some allies, work with the schools to examine their policies on homework and extracurricular activities. How much is enough? When do we reach the point of diminishing returns? When are we driven by guilt, and when by a reasonable expectation that all of this busyness will help?

In the same vein, examine the practices at your workplace. Keep in mind that you are not the only person who has a family. Your co-workers have obligations as well, and will probably appreciate your raising these issues. (Again, look for like-minded people. Don't go it alone.) Don't alienate people, but don't feel that you have to be on the defensive. Compared to most other industrialized nations, the United States has family policies that seem Dickensian.

In the area of food, think about bringing back some form of home economics. Give kids a chance to learn about culinary and consumer skills.

Find the scheduling monsters and rustle them back into their corners. Consider the examples of football in Wayzata, at both the elementary school and the high school level. Be clear about your priorities. Be consistent. Maintain your commitment.

It has taken a generation for our society's underwriting of family meals/family time to plummet. I think there has been a convergence of factors: the restructuring of the workplace, a sense of economic insecurity that we act out through our children (although in a new way: Previous generations insisted on their children having after-school jobs, where we require after-school sports), a pervasive fear about our communities, so that we are reluctant to let our children roam around on our streets, through our backyards. If you look at the fascinating book *The Culture of Fear*, by Barry Glassner, you can see that it is not the actual danger level that has increased, but rather our level of anxiety.

At the same time, we are witnessing a splintering of the national culture, an awareness of our diversity that makes us reluctant to impose our values on anyone else. Some of this is laudable. But again, one of the results has been to pull supports out from under the family.

Eating supper with your family will not create Utopia. But it will help you see what is possible. It will give you a focus, a doable, manageable place to start.

IF YOU CAN'T

Although I have spent this book ranting about supper, you may have noticed that, underneath it all, supper is not really the point. Supper is only the occasion, the excuse. The subject is actually family — establishing, enjoying, and maintaining ties. The goal is creating and reinforcing a secure place for your loved ones in a society that can seem awfully uninterested in human needs.

Our nightly coming together is about the stories created and repeated across space and time, the stories that define us, give us strength, and hold us together. And it is about food, through which all these exchanges take place. So what if, after convincing you of the importance of family supper, you find that you can't do it now, or at all? First, be alive to making choices. Be alert to whatever opportunities come your way. Do your best to direct them your way. Stay on the lookout for possibilities of change.

If you just can't do supper, find ways to incorporate its benefits into other family activities. How about breakfast, or a late-night snack? In one family, where the father comes home late, everyone gathers together for a snack and a chat they have named Last Call. How about Sunday dinner, or Saturday brunch? If you can settle on a time with cultural, ethnic, or familial ties, it will be that much stronger. For Jewish families, Shabbat supper is a ready-made refresher, the place where, for a moment, time stands still. But whatever you choose, the important ideas are intention and consistency. Make sure your family knows that this is what you are doing, and that it is important. They don't have to love it; they just have to do it.

Whatever you settle on, use the occasion to talk to your family members, and to listen. This is not the time for heavy-duty lessons, recriminations, stony silences, or hogging the conversation. Have everyone check in, and then go from there, asking questions that are open ended, nonjudgmental. If your kids aren't responding to *What did you do today*, it may be that you need to listen more closely to what's important in their lives, which doesn't always mean the deep things. Talk about shared hobbies, proclivities, activities. Remember the past, plan for the future. Get reports from the field. Be serious, be silly, be hot, be cold. Be who you are, although, hopefully, a good version of that.

One family that sociologist Kerry Daly interviewed sets aside Saturday morning. They go out for breakfast, get out of the house, shift gears. You might reasonably point out that this is contrary to the idea that I have been pushing — staying at home, doing it yourself — but the more immediate goal is to give your family an occasion they can count on. If you can't have supper every night, make a point of doing it when you can. If supper is out of the question, try breakfast. If you can't have breakfast, play Parcheesi. If you can't even find that much time to be with each other, it's time for some serious assessment of what *together* means for your group.

I have tried to help you become more aware without laying on one more guilt trip or adding one more set of demands. If this all feels like too much, I hope you will reassess your schedule in its entirety. See what is, in fact, essential. Again, use the memory test. Years from now, what will your children remember of their childhoods? Which parts will you recall with warmth; which with embarrassment? What are the warm spots you remember from your own childhood? How would you like your days to play out starting now, into the future?

Last night my husband and I did not eat supper together. In thirty years of marriage, this is nothing unusual. But perhaps because I am writing this book, when I stood in the kitchen by myself, microwaving my little plastic container of leftover stir-fry, I felt a wave of depression. Our kitchen — which has been factory, salon, study hall, café, command center, cozy nook, parlor, the place where we huddle around the woodstove when the power goes out — seemed heartless and shoddy, the kind of room where sad people only shuffle through.

All this because of one night's missed supper? Let me explain:

I had been having one of those patches when the things that sometimes don't bother me at all about my husband had taken center stage in my mind. They're the sorts of things you can live with easily enough for years. Then they rise to consciousness and you can't shake them, like a song you don't like but keep humming. Worse, they're not the kind of things that you, or your spouse, can do much about.

There hadn't been a fight; things hadn't even escalated to the point where one of us said, *We have to talk*, or, *Well, you've sure been in a bad mood*. We had both been busy; comings and goings, the normal things.

Standing alone in front of the microwave, I realized how soothing it is to know that most nights we will sit down together and face each other. Not that I normally think about it; it's just part of my day. But it's there, like the way, in fall and winter, I can see the sunset (not the sun exactly, just the red sky, brilliant) out the window above the kitchen sink.

Sometimes we have lots of things we want to talk about. Other nights it's just the occasional phrase. What's new? Not that much from day to day. Do I actually care about the details of his business day? His commute? Whom he had lunch with? I plead the Fifth. Does he really want to know how my research or writing has progressed today? He does not, and I don't blame him. Any news from the kids? The family? Are there social plans to be made? Did something in the news set one of us off?

But last night I would have told Peter about how I had gone to Charlestown for an interview, to what used to be the old navy yard. I hadn't been there in years, not since the kids were little and we used to take them to see Old Ironsides.

(Peter is a sailing nut; Old Ironsides was one of our standard kid outings.) Back then, the navy yard was in the process of being decommissioned. The historic ship was berthed in an unpopulated, eerie space separated from the living city by highway and urban decay. But you could see the clarity of the wonderful brick-and-stone, early-nineteenth-century buildings that lined the military-straight streets. You could look out at the waterfront, the piers jutting out into Boston Harbor. You could imagine all kinds of things.

When I went there yesterday, it was as if our old imaginings had become real. The detritus of centuries had been removed. The fine old buildings had been tastefully rehabbed, as if they had been encouraged to become more themselves, to reveal their square redbrick essence. Inside were academic institutions, businesses, condominiums. Outside were tourists — enough for vitality, not enough to produce gridlock. Having lunch with a friend there overlooking the harbor after my interview felt like a mini vacation. I wanted to tell Peter about all of it. I knew that, in the intervening years he had been to the area often; he worked with the new businesses, the new labs. I wanted to tell him that I had seen the transformation as well.

Supper would have been the obvious time. I could picture us sitting together in our usual seats. I would serve him a nice meal. The room would become brighter, cheerier. It would smell better because I would be cooking something tasty and healthful, something we would enjoy together.

Supper is about prevention and repair. We don't have to reinvent our relationships every day, because they are already built into what we know we will do. We don't have to make a special time to get together, because it already exists. We have a place where we can bring things, a set of actions that is both symbolic and real.

There is an old story told about a great seventeenth-century rabbi, the Ba'al Shem-Tov. It is said that, when the Jews were threatened by misfortune, he would go to a certain part of the forest to meditate. He would light a fire, say a prayer, and, lo and behold, a miracle would happen.

In time, the great rabbi died. Later, when the Jews were threatened, his disciple would go to the same place in the forest and address God: "I do not know how to light the fire, but I still know the prayer." And the miracle would happen.

Eventually, this rabbi died as well. In the era of *his* disciple, when the Jews were threatened, the rabbi would go into the forest. "I do not know how to light the fire, I no longer remember the prayer, but at least I know how to come to the right place."

We are at a time when many of us have lost the meditation, the prayer, and the fire. At least we still know where to come. For families, that place is called home.

A Selection of Blessings

Good food, good meat,
Good God, let's eat!

May the Lord accept this, our offering, and bless our
food that it may bring us strength in our body, vigor
in our mind, and selfless devotion in our heart for his
service.

— Swami Paramanda, *Book of Daily Thoughts and Prayer*

ROUND (SUNG)
Oh give thanks, oh give thanks,
Oh give thanks unto the Lord
For he is gracious and his mercy endureth,
Endureth forever.

ROUND (SUNG)
For health and strength and daily food
We praise thy name, O Lord.

We thank the Lord above
for the food we are about to receive
for the blessings of the past week
and the week to come.
Keep us well and happy.

Rub a dub dub. Thanks for the grub.

This food is the gift of the Earth, the Sky, the
  Whole Universe and much hard work.
May we live in such a way as to be worthy to receive it.
May we transform our unskillful states of mind and
  learn to eat in moderation.
May we eat only foods which nourish us and
  promote good health.
We accept this food in order to realize the practice
  of peace and understanding.

— Buddhist Blessing

Bless us oh Lord and these thy gifts which we are
  about to receive from thy bounty.

JOHNNY APPLESEED SONG
The Lord is good to me
For this I thank the Lord
For giving me the things I need
The sun, the rain and the appleseed
The Lord is good to me.

For food in a world where many walk in hunger;
For faith in a world where many walk in fear;
For friends in a world where many walk alone;
We give you thanks, O Lord.

For all we eat, and all we wear,
For daily bread, and nightly care,
we thank thee, heavenly Father.

Good Lord — Bless these sinners as they eat their
   dinners.

Thank you for the food we eat,
Thank you for the world so sweet,
Thank you for the birds that sing,
Thank you God for everything.

Blessed are you, lord our God, ruler of the universe,
who brings forth bread from the earth.

— Hebrew blessing

Blessed are you, Lord our God, ruler of the universe,
who feeds the entire world with goodness, with
grace, with kindness, and with mercy.

— Hebrew after-meal prayer

What to Talk About

AIM FOR A mixture: housekeeping details, reports on each person's day, stories, plans, reminiscences, jokes, big-topic questions.

No fights. No hot-button topics. Include fun topics, jokes, stories, as well as paying attention to events outside the family including politics, sports, and local happenings. This is the time to, in some ways, bring kids and adults to the same level. Engage each other by being imaginative, not invasive.

If you are a game family, or a memorizing family, this is your time: state capitals, models of cars, sports teams.

When you are asking kids about their day's experience, remember to scaffold: Give them help about what kinds of things are appropriate or interesting.

With small children, especially, pay attention to language — yours and theirs. Encourage talk about the past and the future. Explain new words.

Use this family time as an occasion to talk about the extended family. Share stories from your own childhood, youth, young adulthood.

It's not always a question of talking, but of airspace. The person who is taking a turn might not want to have to talk at every moment, but might want some time to compose her thoughts. Be careful not to let the big talkers monopolize the conversation. Some families do this formally, with an object (a talking stick; a special stone that each person puts out in front of his space when he wants to talk). Some families do this metaphorically.

Maureen Treacy Lahr and Julie Pfitzinger, friends in Minneapolis–St. Paul, put together a spiral-bound book of conversation starters for family meals called *Keep Talking*. Questions include:

- How would you describe your best friend to someone who's never met her before?
- If you could create a new law, what would it be about and why?
- Describe your soul. What happens to your soul when you die?
- Describe the most exciting moment of your life so far!
- If you could rename yourself, what name would you choose?"

Some of my own questions include:

- What was the most embarrassing thing that ever happened to you?
- What is your earliest memory?
- Where would you really love to live — country, city, or in between? What kind of neighborhood, what kind of house?

Encourage all family members to come up with their own questions. Also encourage them to respect the interests, ideas, and opinions of the others at the table.

— BIBLIOGRAPHY —

1. WELL, MAGIC ENOUGH . . .

Hofferth, Sandra L., and John F. Sandberg (University of Michigan). "How American Children Spend Their Time." *Journal of Marriage and Family* 63 (May 2001): 295–308.

2. MAKING THE FRAME

Daly, Kerry J. "Deconstructing Family Time." *Journal of Marriage and Family* 63 (May 2001): 283–294.

Shore, Bradd. *Family Time: Studying Myth and Ritual in Working Families.* Emory Center for Myth and Ritual in American Life, Working Paper No. 27, May 2003.

3. HOW EATING SUPPER MAKES US STRONG

Anorexia Nervosa and Related Eating Disorders (ANRED) Web site: www.anred.com.

Brody, Jane. "Peril of the Night: When Calories Come Calling." *New York Times* (April 20, 2004).

Duke, Marshall P., Robyn Fivush, Amber Lazarus, and Jennifer Bohanek (Department of Psychology, Emory University). *Of Ketchup and Kin: Dinnertime Conversations as a Major Source of Family Knowledge, Family Adjustment, and Family Resilience.* Emory Center for Myth and Ritual in American Life, Working Paper No. 26, May 2003.

Markson, Samia, and Barbara H. Fiese. "Family Rituals as a Protective Factor for Children with Asthma." *Journal of Pediatric Psychology* 25, No. 7 (2000): 471–479.

"National Longitudinal Study of Adolescent Health." *Journal of the American Medical Association* 278, No. 10 (September 10, 1997): 830.

"National Survey of American Attitudes on Substance Abuse." These yearly surveys are available from the National Center on Addiction and Substance Abuse (CASA) at Columbia University.

Steinglass, Peter, with Linda A. Bennett, Steven J. Wolin, and David Reiss. *The Alcoholic Family.* New York: Basic Books, 1987.

4. WHO, WHAT, WHERE

Arendell, Teresa. "The New Care Work of Middle Class Mothers." In *Minding the Time in Family Experience,* Volume 3 (Oxford: Elsevier Science, 2001), pages 163–204.

Bond, James, Ellen Galinsky, and Jennifer Swanberg. *The 1997 National Study of the Changing Workforce.* New York: Families and Work Institute, 1997, page 38.

Brownell, Kelly D., and Katherine Battlen Horgen. *Food Fight.* New York: McGraw-Hill, 2004.

Children's Nutrition Research Center study: bcm.edu/cnrc/consumer/archives/tveating.htm.

Colwin, Laurie. *More Home Cooking.* New York: HarperCollins, 1993.

Cutler, David, Edward Glaesner, and Jesse Shapiro. *Why Have Americans Become More Obese?* Cambridge, Mass.: National Bureau of Economic Research, Working Paper 9446, 2003.

Daly, Kerry J. "Controlling Time in Families." In *Minding the Time in Family Experience,* Volume 3 (Oxford: Elsevier Science, 2001), pages 227–249.

Elias, Norbert. *The History of Manners.* New York: Urizen Books, 1978.

———. *The Civilizing Process.* Oxford, UK, and Malden, Mass.: Blackwell Publishers, 2000.

Finkelstein, Joanne. *Dining Out.* Oxford: Polity Press, 1989.

Fisher, M. F. K. *The Art of Eating.* New York: Macmillan, 1990.

Garber, Marjorie. *Sex and Real Estate.* New York: Pantheon Books, 2000.

Harris, Marvin. *Good to Eat.* New York: Simon & Schuster, 1987.

Hofferth, Sandra, and Jack Sandberg. "Changes in American Children's Time, 1981–1997." *PSID Child Development Supplement,* University of Michigan (2000).

Larson, Reed. "Mothers' Time in Two-Parent and One-Parent Families." In *Minding the Time in Family Experience,* Volume 3 (Oxford: Elsevier Science, 2001), pages 85–109.

Putnam, Robert D. *Bowling Alone.* New York: Simon & Schuster, 2000.

Rozin, Paul. "Psychological Perspectives on Food Preferences and Avoidances." In *Food and Evolution* by Marvin Harris and Eric B. Ross (Philadelphia: Temple University Press, 1987).

———. "Sociocultural Influences on Human Food Selection." In *Why We Eat What We Eat,* edited by Elizabeth D. Capaldi (Washington, D.C.: American Psychological Association, 1996).

———. "Food Is Fundamental, Fun, Frightening, and Far-Reaching." *Social Research* 66 (1999): 9–30.

Rozin, Paul, Kimberly Kabnick, Erin Pete, Claude Fischler, and Christy Shields. "The Ecology of Eating." *Psychological Science* 14, No. 5 (September 2003).

Rybczynski, Witold. *Home: A Short History of an Idea.* New York: Viking Penguin, 1986.

Visser, Margaret. *The Rituals of Dinner.* New York: Penguin Books, 1991.

Warde, Alan, and Lydia Martens. *Eating Out.* Cambridge and New York: Cambridge University Press, 2000.

5. NOURISHMENT

Davis, Clara M. "Can Babies Choose Their Food?" *Parents Magazine* (January 1930).

Eisenberg, Marla, Rachel E. Olson, Dianne Neumark-Sztainer, Mary Story, and Linda H. Bearinger. "Correlations Between Family Meals and Psychosocial Well-Being Among Adolescents." *Archives of Pediatrics and Adolescent Medicine* (August 2004).

Fredericks, Lynn. *Cooking Time Is Family Time.* New York: William Morrow, 1999.

Gillman, Matthew W., Sheryl L. Rifas-Shiman, A. Lindsay Frazier, Helaine Rocket, Carlos A. Camargo Jr., Alison E. Field, Catherine S. Berkey, and Graham A. Colditz. "Family Dinner and Diet Quality Among Older Children and Adolescents." *Archives of Family Medicine* (2000): 9.

Neumark-Sztainer, Dianne, Peter J. Hannah, Mary Story, Jillian Croll, and Cheryl Perry. "Family Meal Patterns." *Journal of the American Dietetic Association* 103, No. 3 (March 2003).

Neumark-Sztainer, Dianne, Mary Story, Diann Ackard, Jillian Moe, and Cheryl Perry. "The Family Meal." *Journal of Nutrition Education* 32, No. 6 (November–December 2000).

———. "Family Meals Among Adolescents." *Journal of Nutrition Education* 32, No. 6 (November–December 2000).

Satter, Ellyn. *How to Get Your Kid to Eat . . . But Not Too Much.* Palo Alto, Calif.: Bull Publishing, 1987.

———. *Secrets of Feeding a Healthy Family.* Madison, Wis.: Kelcy Press, 1999.

Story, Mary, and Judith E. Brown. "Do Young Children Instinctively Know What to Eat?" *New England Journal of Medicine* 316, No. 2 (January 8, 1987).

6. SPIRIT AND FLESH

Huebsch, Bill. *Handbook for Success in Whole Community Catechesis.* Mystic, Conn.: Twenty-third Publications, 2004.

Mogel, Wendy. *The Blessing of a Skinned Knee: Using Jewish Teachings to Raise Self-Reliant Children.* New York: Scribner, 2001.

7. THROUGH ALL THE YEARS

Imber-Black, Evan, and Janine Roberts. *Rituals for Our Times.* New York: HarperCollins, 1993.

Imber-Black, Evan, Janine Roberts, and Richard Whiting. *Rituals in Families and Family Therapy.* New York: W. W. Norton, 1988.

8. REPORTS FROM THE FIELD

Dickinson, David K., and Patton O. Tabors. *Beginning Literacy with Language.* Baltimore: Paul H. Brookes Publishing, 2002.

Doherty, William J. *The Intentional Family.* New York: Avon Books, 1997.

———. *Take Back Your Kids.* Notre Dame, Ind.: Sorin Books, 2000.

Doherty, William J., and Barbara Z. Carlson. *Putting Family First.* New York: Henry Holt, 2002.

Lahr, Maureen Treacy, and Julie Pfitzinger. *Keep Talking.* Edina, Minn.: Beavers Pond Press, 2003.

Rosenfeld, Alvin, and Nicole Wise. *Hyper-Parenting.* New York: St. Martin's Press, 2000.

Snow, Catherine E., Susan Burns, and Peg Griffin. *Preventing Reading Difficulties in Young Children.* Washington, D.C.: National Academy Press, 1998.

9. MAKING IT BETTER

Bower, Dee Sarton, and Mary Eileen Wells. *Homemade to Go: The Complete Guide to Co-op Cooking.* Meridian, Ind.: Purrfect Publishing, 1997.

Fitzsimmons, William, Marlyn McGrath Lewis, and Charles Ducey. *Time Out or Burn Out for the Next Generation.* Office of Admissions and Financial Aid, Harvard University, 2001.

Glassner, Barry. *The Culture of Fear.* New York: Basic Books, 1999.